Stitched Textiles
Birds

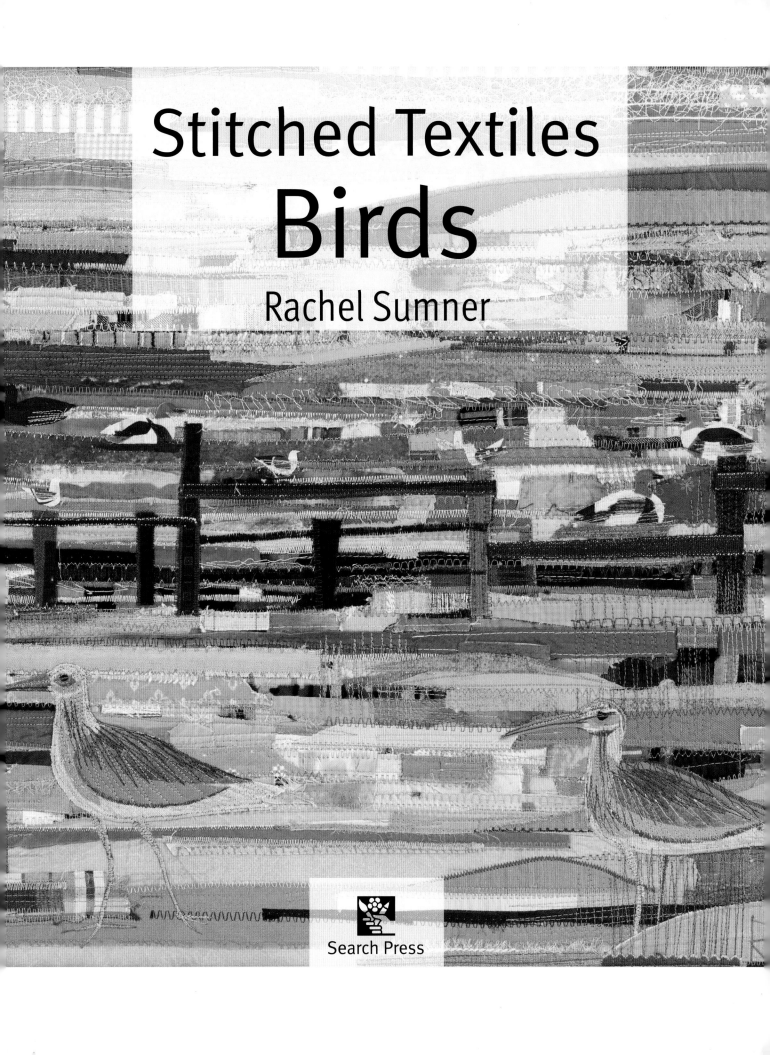

Stitched Textiles
Birds

Rachel Sumner

Search Press

First published in Great Britain 2016

Search Press Limited
Wellwood, North Farm Road,
Tunbridge Wells, Kent TN2 3DR

ISBN: 978-1-84448-988-6

Suppliers
If you have difficulty in obtaining
any of the materials or equipment
mentioned in this book, then please
visit the Search Press website for
details of suppliers:
www.searchpress.com

Printed in China

Dedication

To the two Mabels – my maternal and paternal grandmothers –
who always engaged in some sort of textile project. For my mother
Dorothy, with her love of stitchery, the natural world and those
many years of making and mending for her family, and to her sister
Mu for adding her appreciation of all things arty.

Front cover
Swallows; see also page 91.

Page 1
The Fountain; see also page 65.

Pages 2–3
Shoreline; see also pages 96–97.

Pages 4–5
Smallholding; see also page 62.

Contents

Introduction

I would describe myself as an artist who uses textile techniques. I live and work in North Devon, where the coast and landscape have a strong influence on my artistic life. Walking, collecting from the beach and observing what goes on around me informs much of what happens back in the studio. I also love colour and the challenge of recreating what I see from my collection of recycled fabrics and material acquisitions. It is my own parallel universe where my imaginings and preoccupations are translated into collage and stitch, with hopefully a touch of humour as well. As well as textile work, I also make assemblages from driftwood and other finds. There is definite cross-fertilisation between the two activities, with found materials appearing in my embroideries and textile bits and pieces regularly featuring on my assemblages.

I have a degree in fine art painting but was more interested in cutting up and reassembling my work and experimenting with various textile techniques than being a serious painter. Looking back, it has been something of a journey to find a medium that suited me. After many years of not using my art training other than in a domestic setting, the conviction grew in me that I should try to take up some form of artistic activity again. In a bid to get started in some way I got involved in surface decoration – hand painting on textiles – something which grew into a full-time occupation. Several years on I felt the pull to put more self-expression into my work and began to make pictures from the fabrics that I had hoarded over the years. This included vintage fabrics collected while living in France, years of charity shop finds and some of the experimental dyeing that I had done at college. Whereas a blank piece of paper or canvas had felt like a barrier to being creative, a pile of fabric seemed to contain a much happier prospect for experimentation and expression. If in the end the experiment didn't quite work, then it was returned to the scrap bag to be reinvented another day.

The notion of craftsmanship and physically making and shaping materials in tandem with developing and refining an idea is something that works for me. A story builds in my head as I get involved with handling the materials. Bound up with this is the use of recycled materials and the pleasure of making something new from old. I feel that just like certain foods or music, textiles can be a window on the past, evoking memories of events and details of our former lives that we thought were forgotten. On handling a fabric with a colour combination, pattern, touch or smell similar to one from the past it can transport us to another place and time. I still remember the feel as well as my attitude towards some of the clothes and textiles of my youth. The fabric bits and pieces one collects and gathers around are not random but informed by a lifelong relationship to textiles. This adds another layer of interest to the creative process; the resonances of the materials themselves. There is always an interesting conversation to be had with other textile enthusiasts around their fabric collections and how they relate to them.

The subject of my producing a book on stitched textiles arose when I was immersed in a series of work featuring the sea. Whether to stick with what I know or find something different? A few birds had appeared here and there in my work so I took it as a wonderful opportunity to explore a developing theme. The presence of birds enlivens any landscape or garden scene and I have always been aware of their capacity to amuse or move me in some way. This was the perfect excuse to delve into another world with new colours, shapes, characters and a multitude of settings to place them in. The approach and techniques used in this book could be applied to almost any subject that you might wish to capture in stitch. I hope my enjoyment of both birds and textiles is conveyed in the work that follows.

Petal

23 x 23cm (9 x 9in)

A still life of favourite things: a blue jug, anemones and a chaffinch. I set up my sewing machine in front of the jug and flowers and stitched from life – I was trying to capture each individual flower and not treat them all in the same way. I used my imagination to introduce a bird from my garden to the scene. This piece uses appliqué with machine embroidery.

Flood Waters

50 x 50cm (19¾ x 19¾in)

A walk on Christmas day when the water meadows of my home town were flooded is the inspiration for this picture. Canada geese drifted about on the transformed landscape calling to each other with their haunting voices. This piece features appliqué with machine embroidery.

Materials

Your fabric library

Calling the collection of fabrics that I have accumulated over the years and which are housed in plastic bags and storage boxes a 'library' may sound a little grandiose but I think of it in this way because it is my primary resource and a constant point of reference. As well as providing me with inspiration, fabric is also the medium in which I work and express my ideas. Organising your collection in some meaningful way will facilitate your projects and maximise your options. Colour is perhaps the most obvious way to order fabrics for collage and appliqué purposes; regrouping and restoring order to my 'library' is one of my rituals at the successful completion of a project and in preparation for the next.

For the projects in this book, fabrics are not only an inspiration but also the main source of colour. In order to mix and blend colours in the way that you might with paint, you will need a good range of fabrics to work from. Most of us with an interest in textiles already have some sort of fabric collection waiting for the right project to come along. If you feel you have insufficient, just get hold of a few extra fabrics to bridge any gaps. Sourcing fabrics needn't be expensive; off-cuts from furnishing and dressmaking projects, donations from friends, remnants, old clothing, charity shop oddments and pattern books form the core of my collection. Bear in mind when choosing, that beyond colour and pattern, fabrics also have their own intrinsic properties that need to be taken into consideration such as weight, fibre content, texture and surface.

When starting out on a project, one of the first things I do is to sort through my fabrics, amassing a large pile of likely colours and patterns that might be of use. I will reject and refine these choices as I go along, often returning for more, as an idea develops. The fabrics I use are nearly all natural fibres: cotton, linen and silk. This is my personal choice; I find them easy to handle and fairly resilient to the rough treatment they get from being cut, stitched, steam-ironed and transformed into fabric pictures. Another advantage is that these fibres can all be dyed with easy-to-use procion dyes, which is useful if I am seeking to either modify or create a new colour for a specific project. There are of course many innovative and exciting mixed and synthetic fabrics available, and as long as they can withstand some heat and being overworked by a sewing machine, they should be fine for use. Some of my fabrics are of unknown fibre content, but if it looks right and handles well it is definitely worth trying.

A selection of my blue-toned fabrics, with a range of different textures, patterns and weights.

Threads

Although at times your thread will be used for stitching down and securing fabrics with the minimum of visual impact, by and large, the selection and use of thread should be regarded as an opportunity to add something to your work. Use it as a drawing tool for putting the finishing touches to a picture, for shaping and defining your appliqué compositions, or for its coloration – to blend in or highlight. Imaginative use of thread and stitching can be used to great effect and will make a great difference to how a picture turns out, so it is worth spending a bit of time considering your options. When you have made your choice of thread, try it against your piece of work to double check it's right.

Much of my artwork reflects the fact that I am a bit of a magpie. This extends itself into the realm of threads, which have been acquired in the same way as many of my fabrics – by serendipity. As a result I have a large thread collection that contains lots of different qualities and makes. Through trying them on different projects, favourites have emerged and I have expanded my colour range in these brands. With the wealth of specialised threads for sewing and embroidery on sale, it is worth trying a selection to see how they perform on your machine before investing in a whole colour range. The big test is whether they are strong enough to withstand the rigours of machine embroidery. Thread that breaks easily can be very frustrating when in the middle of a picture.

I mostly use a quality, general use polyester thread because of its strength and durability. For surface effects I have a core of useful colours in a more lustrous rayon 'machine embroidery' range but have found that these are a bit more fragile and need careful handling, especially on mechanical sewing machines. On your machine it may not be a problem; it is one of those things that only experience will tell. Thread can be quite an expensive aspect of embroidery and it's worth seeking out online suppliers and investing in larger spools of a much-used colour. They can always be decanted onto spare bobbins.

My choice of colours is augmented by the miscellaneous collection of cottons and other threads acquired over the years. I will also use these to mix up different types of thread at times, seeing what thick with thin or contrasting colours will bring. The stitches can distort slightly bringing the bobbin thread onto the surface with interesting results. Colour is usually the priority when selecting a thread for textile pictures so, like my fabrics, I try to keep them in colour groupings. Because it is my most-used colour, I have a whole drawer full of blues, then a couple of shoe boxes for reds and yellows and greens and earth colours. It's all a question of easy access and being able to see what you have.

For hand-finishing details such as eyes, beaks and feet I use single strands of stranded embroidery silks.

Found objects

Old sewing boxes and other haberdashery remnants handed down or found in charity shops are a window into a past life, when people used to routinely make their own clothes, hoarding old buttons, recycling zips and patching and repairing. I still have items from my own family's sewing boxes, which are no longer of any practical use but that I can still remember in the hands of their owners. For nostalgic reasons as well as their decorative qualities, I sometimes like to incorporate one or two of these items into my work, adding a personal subtext. It might be an old sewing needle packet, a zip, a card of pop fasteners, or a label from a wooden cotton reel that gets selected. This has extended to more recently acquired 'treasures': jewel-coloured sweet wrappers, clothing trims, postage stamps or fragments of fishing line and netting from the beach. There is no limitation on using such articles, other than the technical difficulty of securing them. It might be a good idea to start out cautiously as far as using a sewing machine is concerned and add in any found objects by hand-stitching them in place at the end.

With birds as our subject matter, stamps with a nature theme work well as part of a background patchwork. Bits of labels and text can also be interesting. Other items might be used for their colouring, rather than for what they actually are. Why not create a tree trunk from a zip fastener, or use buttons as flower centres? Incorporating found objects is a way of being quite abstract and suggesting a theme or scene without being literal. What do you hoard? Being playful and adventurous in the early stages of a piece of work can be great for getting started. The pleasure of just putting things together in a light-hearted and intuitive way can bring freshness to your work and inspire new ideas.

Equipment

Sewing equipment

Sewing machine

A sewing machine is essential for the projects in this book, but it doesn't have to be an expensive one. With a bit of imagination, even a basic model can create wonderful results. Straight and zigzag stitching used creatively can do a lot, but having a machine with at least a small range of embroidery stitches can be useful. Sophisticated computerised models tend to have a lot more functions but may need more delicate handling; a mechanical model may be more robust and cope more easily with the layers of fabric. It's a case of balancing all your requirements from a sewing machine: soft furnishings, dressmaking and creative. Make learning your sewing machine's capabilities an opportunity to experiment and play around with combinations of fabrics and stitches. It will help you come up with imaginative ways of using what functions your machine has and avoid annoying mistakes halfway through a project. This is discussed more fully in the techniques section. Cleaning the accumulations of lint, oiling and a regular service in line with the manual's instructions are important and part of your routine care.

Feet

For embroidery and appliqué, a special embroidery foot may be available for your model of machine. This usually takes the form of an acrylic, see-through presser foot that enables you to monitor fine detail as you stitch. A modern machine may have a special free-stitching foot; on older models a darning foot is required for free stitching techniques. In both cases the feed dog is lowered and the fabric moved freely beneath the needle in any direction. This is often used in conjunction with an embroidery ring.

Needles

An inappropriate, blunt or bent sewing machine needle can be the cause of incorrect stitching. Always check with your sewing machine manual for the right ones to use and have spares to hand.

Bobbins

Because machine embroidery calls for many changes of thread colour, extra bobbin cases are very useful to have on hand. The bottom thread doesn't have to match exactly the shade of the top thread but having a selection of colours ready to go can quicken up the process of thread changing. Once the machine is set up for bobbin winding I will fill any empty spares at the same time.

Scissors and other accessories

Scissors play an important role in creative textile work. You will need to be able to cut out accurate shapes. A pair of good dressmaking shears as well as a small pair of sharp scissors for cutting loose threads and intricate details will cover most of your requirements.

A stitch ripper for unpicking, pins and pincushion to hand, along with a hand-sewing kit of needles and embroidery silks for a few finishing touches are also essentials.

Iron-on interfacings and webs

Iron-on interfacing

This lightweight material is used for stiffening collars and lapels in dressmaking but also provides good support when constructing a picture. Background fabrics can be quickly laid out on the interfacing base, then ironed into position when you are happy with your arrangement. Anchoring them in this way removes the need to pin and tack (baste) in readiness for stitching. A medium weight is recommended.

When using stretchy or lightweight fabrics for appliqué, applying lightweight interfacing to the back of the fabric before cutting out will make handling much easier.

Other products like 'stitch and tear' or a firm interfacing without adhesive will also provide a good backing that tolerates a lot of overstitching. Pin or tack (baste) your fabrics into place before stitching in this case.

Fusible web

This is a thin web of adhesive with a parchment backing that is applied to the reverse of fabrics with an iron. Once in position, shapes can be drawn onto the back ready for cutting out (always remembering to draw out the required shape in reverse). The backing is then peeled away allowing the piece to be ironed into place. This can make handling fine fabrics a lot easier, limiting the tendency to fray and keeping the fabrics firmly in position when stitching or embroidering over the top.

Dissolvable fabric

This comes in various forms and is a clear or semi-transparent film. It is useful for free-stitching techniques and when overlaying many pieces of fabric or incorporating found objects into your work. It provides a smooth surface for the machine foot to travel over while keeping all the as-yet unsecured elements in place. Without it, loose threads can catch and fabric pieces can be displaced by the foot, making sewing very difficult. After sewing, the invisible fabric is washed out in cold water leaving no trace.

Other useful items

A cutting mat and scalpel are useful for making templates and mounting your work. The mat grid also helps when marking out finished pieces for trimming down to size and can be used with a rotary cutter for making strips of material. Partner this with a good-quality ruler.

Tracing paper is useful for transferring designs to fabrics and making pattern pieces.

A sketchbook, layout pad, pens and pencils are tools for recording thoughts, designing and refining your ideas. And you will also need an iron and an ironing board.

Tip

When ironing, place your finished work face down on an old towel and place an old tea towel on top, to protect the back from direct contact with the iron. Pressing against an unyielding surface can leave shiny rub marks when there are several thicknesses of fabrics – the surface of the towel will prevent this.

Design

Inspiration

Inspiration for a new piece of work can come at any time. For me it rarely happens when I'm sitting at home with a blank piece of paper to hand – it is much more likely to happen when I'm engaged in some other activity. Jotting the idea down in a few words, taking a photograph or doing a lightning sketch will help keep it in mind. It might be that I wish to 'capture a moment', something seen or experienced; it might be a favourite place I want to commemorate or record, or even a phrase I have heard or read. Later in the workroom, I will sift through these ideas. Although some may have lost their appeal or make little sense with hindsight (this happens to me quite a lot!), one or two will have stuck in my mind and merit further work. The role of design is to pin these ideas down and turn them into a composition that will work in fabric and stitch. It doesn't need to be a lengthy process. Just a few minutes of planning can help avoid simple errors and make a great difference to the outcome of a project.

As well as using bird reference books, I keep a scrapbook full of cuttings from magazines, newspapers and postcards, as well as some of my own drawings and photographs. These are all images that have caught my eye in one way or another. It is roughly divided into sections of interest: garden birds, chickens, dodos, sea birds and so on. It is a great resource for researching birds in different attitudes, such as flying or resting, as well as viewing their markings closely.

Moodboards

When embarking on a new piece of work I will create a moodboard containing fabric swatches, reference photographs, stitch samples, colour combinations and original jottings. I positioned it above my work table so that I can look up from my planning or sewing and have the ideas and inspirations in front of me.

Interpreting the world in fabric and stitch is not an obvious thing to do; you have to make up your own visual language to describe an idea. Using found or pre-existing colours and patterns takes a leap of the imagination, but is also where a lot of the fun and creativity comes in. Having birds as the subject matter also presents its own challenges; one can rarely get right up close to the subject and the nature of the encounter is often fleeting.

Keep in mind just what it is you are trying to capture: the bird in its environment, a behaviour or interaction, or just the bird itself. Try to keep your design simple, as a lot of complexity will come from the fabrics and stitching. More detail can come in at the end if required. Another important consideration is the size you want the finished piece to be and its implications in terms of level of detail and how much of the surroundings you want to include.

Sketching out your ideas

Gather together any available reference material, including any photographs you have taken of the setting, or any jottings made, and try to draw out the idea as a simple line drawing. This can be a very quick sketch – you are just trying to work out what to include and where to position it. In the context of making fabric pictures, most of the drawing is about composition – where things should go on the page – but it is also good for practising the shapes and postures.

If it doesn't look right, consider how the elements fit on the page. Is the format right? Would a square or rectangle shape be better? It may be that quite an imaginative approach is needed in order to get across the original inspiration. You may need to get in closer to the subject or even alter the perspective. Don't be afraid to have several attempts on scrap paper or in a sketchbook in preparation for the finished layout. Part of this process might involve practising the shape and attitude of the bird or birds, something a scrapbook and reference books can be very useful for.

With these considerations in mind, build on your sketch and try to plan the layout. Draw out the size of the finished piece and pencil in your design. Dividing the page into a grid might help you with this, especially if you need to scale up a smaller drawing. As this is all to be translated into fabrics, you are concentrating on outline shapes that will be used to make pattern pieces, with a few indicators of where some of the stitched detail might go.

On this sketchbook page I have been recording seagulls in various stances for an embroidery project. I will pick out individuals as models for my seagulls when making the final layout.

The layout for the starting project is very simple. The idea was 'bird in a flowerbed'. The layout has the position of all the main features: landscape, bird, flowers and insect. The previous quick sketch phase helped develop the stylised bird and flower shapes before arriving at this final arrangement.

17

Using artworks as inspiration

Trips to places such as churches, museums and art galleries can be very inspirational, and over time I have gathered together a large collection of postcards of some of the objects and art that catches my eye. Sometimes these encounters with art from another age have resonances with a current interest or can fascinate and intrigue, meriting some further investigation.

Here are a couple of examples of work that started off in this way. The idea is not simply to reproduce the piece in question but to use it as a starting point for your own personal interpretation.

Discovering the dodo

I used to be a regular visitor to Bristol museum, where they had a dodo on display: a poignant figure that always caused me to stop and look. I wanted to do some sort of picture on the subject but beyond a simple representation, I wasn't quite sure how to go about it. Later I came across some of the images painted by naturalists on board ships exploring foreign lands in the 17th century and my interest was rekindled. These were naive representations; arrangements of wildlife, insects and vegetation against a brightly painted backdrop. In a time before cameras, it was an attempt to record all the new and exotic species for an audience back home. Their freshness captures the wonder of discovery of these new lands and animals. While searching for more of these contemporaneous images and accounts of the dodo, I read that it took only 80 years from their discovery to their extinction. This inspired me to make my own naive portrait of the dodo, one that is part fact and part imagination. It reflects the limited knowledge we have of a subject that is extinct yet lives on in the popular imagination in art, literature and advertising. I wanted the voyager's ship to be part of the picture; it is anchored offshore while the dodo looks on from his vantage point in the foreground. The bird's shape and plumage were derived from clues from faded specimens and portraits. The imagined nest is threatened by rising water: a metaphor for a disappearing world.

Harvest jug

North Devon has a long pottery tradition dating back to medieval times. Some of the most beautiful examples are harvest jugs from the 17th and 18th centuries, produced by small potteries. These were typically slipware with sgrafitto decoration; pictures and inscriptions created by scratching into a slip coating and revealing the reddish clay beneath. They often feature birds, floral themes or boat scenes, reflecting the importance of rural and maritime influences on the locality. They are both works of art and social documents. My picture celebrates these wonderful artefacts, and brings to life the decoration on the pot in a humorous way. The pot records the stylised renditions of flowers and birds of the original; the top half of the picture then bursts into colourful flowers while in the foreground I have a pigeon looking at his pottery counterparts.

This is the harvest jug that inspired my embroidery.

Using colour

At first glance, creating colour using fabric could be seen as a rather crude means of expression, rather like trying to paint a picture exclusively with colours that come direct from tubes of paint. However, I see it as a process of creative translation. It is a very satisfying feeling to recreate an effect solely with your imagination and a bag of fabrics; it is an interesting and intuitive way of working involving much trial and error.

Awareness of the strengths and limitations of the technique will help you to achieve the best results. You can make a virtue of the fact that it is an arrangement of flat pre-coloured shapes, or disguise it by judicious use of your fabrics and threads. With a still life, I may be drawn to using a flattened perspective and concentrate on making an interesting arrangement of shapes and patterned fabrics. A scene from real life may require a subtler, more realistic approach to form and colour.

Once I have a layout in place, the first step is to gather a pile of fabrics together which might be suitable for the project. Colour is of the first importance, combined with texture and lustre. Bear in mind that dyeing to create or modify certain colours can greatly increase your colour range and may be easier than trying to track down a specific colour. Patterned fabrics may be an attractive proposition at first sight but need to be judged in relation to your other fabric choices. A patterned fabric seen close to can give a very different effect when viewed at a distance. Bold patterns can easily dominate while small patterns or checks can produce subtle effects when subsumed into a design. Remember to take a step back from your work now and again to see how the fabrics are working together.

Choosing the right colour thread also plays an important role in mixing and blending elements in your picture. It can be used to merge two colours, add light or shadow or be neutral. In the first instance, a viewer should see a fabric picture as a whole rather than the sum of its parts. The fact that it is composed of lots of fabric and stitching should then draw in the viewer for a further look.

Above you can see a selection of fabrics from my collection, which contains a huge variety of colours, textures and patterns, as I never quite know when certain pieces will come in handy.

Using fabric

Ideas and inspiration come from many sources – for me, one of these is the fabric itself. Often, without a specific idea in mind, I will start the creative process by going through my fabric odds and ends and seeing what catches my attention. I will piece together groupings and arrangements and quickly sew them together. Some are purely abstract, giving me a chance to play with colours and shapes; other times a fantasy landscape comes into being. It may be a notion of juxtaposing lots of patterned fabrics to see what result that might produce. Once created, these samplers sit around the studio and may get incorporated into another piece of work, inspire a colour scheme or can be developed into a picture idea. I have used lots of these as the backdrop for small bird pictures.

Allowing time to experiment without an end in sight is a good way to develop your fabric skills. You will learn how to balance the fabrics on the page in terms of pattern, texture and colour.

A pathway of patterns. This was an attempt to combine lots of patterned oddments. A restricted colour range and repeating certain fabrics helped it to work. It made me think of a pathway and is awaiting development into a larger piece where I see it as a garden pathway flanked by flat green lawns and some favourite birds hopping about.

Building up a background

Once you have sketched out your ideas, it is important to bring the fabrics you intend to use into the design process. Fabrics are full of pattern, colour and texture that can't be represented on paper. I have a simple technique that I would describe as 'designing on the page': I take my initial sketch and idea, gather up some fabrics, a piece of backing and my scissors, and then compose the background of the picture by a process of trial and error. I observe how the fabrics work together and cut and shape them in response. This way the idea naturally undergoes a refining process as practical considerations come into play. Often, I will start out enthused by the idea of using a particular fabric but seeing it in relation to other fabrics may cause me to reject it – keep an open and questioning mind at this stage. Consider whether there are too many patterns jostling for attention, whether the colour scheme is right or whether the design would benefit from being simplified. (See pages 20–21 for more ideas.)

Once the background is completely covered in blocks of colour, with no white showing through, you have a springboard from which to build up your picture. The next stage is to secure the fabrics in place with some imaginative stitching, and to add in further background elements to create a more convincing landscape, softening the straight lines and breaking up the blocks of colour.

Using the sketch I created on page 17, of a bird in a flowerbed, pages 22–25 will take you through the design process for this simple project. You will be able to see how I build up the scene, add in foreground elements and the bird, and stitch to complete. Throughout this exercise, try to focus on your enjoyment of fabrics and colour, and create combinations that are pleasing to you.

1 Using a piece of interfacing as a base, I experimented with different arrangements of coloured and patterned fabrics and decided on a simple patchwork landscape. I chose a plain blue for the distant sky, an expanse of striped green for the extending middle-distance, and then a range of checked, striped and floral patterns for the foreground. Iron the fabric strips into position once you are happy with them.

2 The next stage is to add in some further fabric details to soften the blocks of colour and to introduce other elements within the landscape. Experiment with fabrics and patterns to see which complement your arrangement. I chose a fine blue and white check for some fluffy clouds on the horizon, striped, tartan and plain green fabrics for some rolling hills, and a textured silk dupion for the pathway.

3 Secure all the fabric elements with decorative stitching. Here you can see that most of the effort has gone into making sure I am happy with the far distance, as apart from a bit of fine detail, this part of the picture is finished. The foreground will be largely covered up by the bird and flowers, so apart from using some nice stitches to secure the fabrics, there is no point in adding any more features at this stage.

Creating foreground elements

Once the background is in place, take a step back and have a good look at what you have created. With colour and mood now sketched out in material, it is time to think about what fabrics you want to set against this; you might want to keep with muted tones or you might want to bring attention to the foreground with some brighter colours. For me, contrast won out. I returned with the background in hand to my fabric collection to find some bright colours to use.

The next stage is to make the bird, butterfly and flowers. With this project, the concern is not about producing a likeness to a particular type of bird or flower but more about producing a pleasing composition using nice bold shapes and colours. After a bit of practice on paper, I made some templates by quickly drawing simple bird, butterfly and flower outlines onto some thin scrap card (see page 123 if you want to use the same shapes). These were cut out and then traced around, on the backs of my chosen fabrics. Using just a simple shape for the flowers will give you scope to play with variations on the pink, red and yellow colour scheme. It is always a good idea to cut out more flowers than you think you will need, in a variety of fabrics. This way you can experiment with the layout and work out by trial and error what looks best. I chose a light base colour for the bird, with a contrasting wing and a bright breast and beak.

4 Pull out a range of contrasting fabrics and work out which will work well against your background. Use the templates on page 123 to create the flowers, butterfly, bird and wing, and cut them out from the fabrics. Simple template shapes put the focus on the fabrics – many of these were selected from off-cuts from previous projects. This is a good way of using up smaller scraps that are already backed with fusible adhesive.

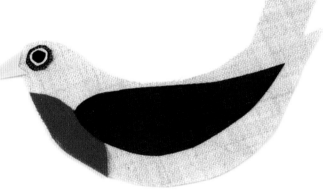

5 Use the templates on page 123 to cut out all the bird's features from fabric backed with fusible adhesive. Arrange the elements in place, then iron to secure.

6 Position the bird against the background and work out where you want it to sit. Iron it gently in place – try to leave the edges of the bird unironed, so that you can slip flowers underneath the edges if need be.

23

Stitching

Your stitching will take place in stages, as you work out your composition. Start by stitching selected areas in the centre of the bird: I stitched the wing and tail. You will then experiment with the flower shapes to work out how the whole composition will come together. You won't finish stitching your bird until you have decided how the flowers will be arranged, in case you wish to slide some underneath the bird before you stitch it, to create an impression of depth. If in doubt, keep stepping back and looking at the overall arrangement before you go any further.

7 Use a burnt orange-coloured thread to draw in some detail on the tail feathers and wing – I used several lines of straight stitch, along with a close-set zigzag edge along the top of the wing.

8 Experiment with several of your flowers and work out if there are any that you wish to slide underneath the bird before you start stitching. Here, I used a large pink flower at the bird's breast, and two small blue flowers at the tail. When you are happy that all the flowers are in place, start to stitch. Use a close-set zigzag stitch to outline the underside of the bird. Change to a lighter shade of brown and continue with the close-set zigzag along the top of the bird from the head to the tail. Use a straight stitch and a dark shade of red to embroider the breast (see finished piece, right, for detail).

Tip
Although it is good to have variations in colour amongst the flowers, having some repeats is also important. The small blue flowers were simple cut-outs added when looking at the arrangement to give more depth to the picture.

Final touches

With the stitching on your bird complete, it is now time to arrange the rest of the flowers. When you arrive at the perfect combination, pin them in place or take a quick reference photograph before stitching them down one by one. You need to work from what would be the furthest to the nearest flower. Use some interesting stitching for the centres and petals as you go along. To help to give light and depth perhaps use two colours of thread on some of the flowers. Finally, the butterfly is added.

9 Play around with your remaining flowers to create a pleasing composition. Don't be afraid to layer them up or overlap them to create different effects.

10 Stitch all the flowers in position: I used starbursts of straight stitch that radiate from the centre of each flower, but you may wish to try something different. Use the template on page 123 to create a butterfly shape. Position this as you want it, iron it down, and then embroider the antennae and a highlight on the wings.

Adapting a design

On a different day, the same exercise can result in a completely different outcome. With some leftover flowers and a ready-made template, you are equipped to continue experimenting and build on the theme. I did just that, making a softer, more abstract garden scene in which I experimented with free-stitching on the sky and vegetation. I had a go at making some different flower shapes as well as cutting out one or two from printed fabric. For the bird, the same template was used but cut out in black; it was moved from centre stage to appearing at the right-hand side. By tipping it up at an angle and adjusting the beak accordingly, a different character emerges. The template collection you build up as you work your way through the projects will be an excellent resource for future pictures: use both sides to create birds facing different ways.

Fabric selection

Here is a run through of the mainstays of my fabric library:

Cottons: calico (muslin) is an inexpensive and versatile fabric. It comes in various weights and is strong but not too heavy. Usually unbleached, with a natural off-white colour, it is easy to dye and is great used for backgrounds and for creatively mounting your work. Cotton dressmaking and patchwork fabrics are easy to find and come in every shade and pattern. I look for patterns such as simple stripes and ginghams; these are good for evoking landscape elements, field patterns, seas and skies. Beyond fashion fabrics, there are many hobby fabrics out there; if dyeing your own fabrics is impractical, but you like the tie-dyed (shibori) effect, you can buy printed versions.

Furnishing fabrics: these come in a tempting range of beautiful colours and patterns. Bear in mind that in making a fabric picture you will probably be building up several thicknesses of cloth and you don't want to overload your machine – concentrate on the lighter-weight ones.

Silks: although these can be more tricky to use, they bring many qualities to a picture such as luminosity, shine and intensity of colour. There are also some wonderful raw silk fabrics with interesting textures; these are not shiny but matte in appearance. Avoid anything too lightweight. My recommended types would be dupion, which is slightly textured and available in wonderful colours, satin, for its sheen, and crêpe de chine, which has a more subtle sheen and good depth of colour. The latter is easy to dye but has some stretch, making it more difficult to use. See the interfacings section (see page 15) for ways of making difficult fabrics easier to handle.

Linens: have a lovely natural appearance and come in a wide selection of colours and stripes. Again, pick the lighter-weight fabrics.

Plain, patterned or striped?

Keep in mind that you will be putting lots of different fabrics together. In most cases, I would choose lots of plain and simple striped fabrics with a sprinkling of the more richly patterned ones. Large or complex patterns, although often very attractive, need to be used with restraint. If too many patterned fabrics appear in a picture they vie for attention and the overall effect can be too 'busy'. As a result, the picture loses impact as a whole.

Organising your fabric library

Organising your fabric collection into colour sections can be a great aid to picture making. This can be done in a decorative or utilitarian way. For larger pieces, I have baskets tightly packed with folded fabrics leaving a 'spine' of colour showing, enabling me to see what colours I have at a glance. Fruit crates, shoe boxes or plastic storage boxes would serve equally well for this purpose.

The finishing touches

I also keep a separate selection of special fabrics, such as sheers, metallics and luxury fabrics. My collection includes sari silk, netting, organza and silk organza with metallic threads. I use these when I need to make finishing touches towards the end of a project. They often fulfil a certain purpose – usually when some effect of light and shadow is needed. Relatively small amounts of these go a long way.

Using scraps

Making fabric pictures is a great way to use up all those odds and ends
of fabric that tend to accumulate over the years. However, one of the
consequences of doing a lot of this type of work is that it also generates lots
of small pieces and off-cuts – an unruly collection of all shapes and sizes
not big enough to be returned to the main body of the fabric collection.
Tempting as it is to clear the decks after each project, these smaller pieces
will come in useful for future pictures. Moreover, as many of the fabrics
will have been backed with fusible web, it saves time and effort to pull a
ready prepared fabric from the scrap bag when adding the smaller details to
pictures. Having them to hand in a transparent plastic bag will make it easy
to spot what you are looking for. If I have amassed large quantities of fabric
scraps I will colour sort them into several bags. Only the very smallest and
least interesting scraps go in the bin.

Techniques

Dyeing fabrics

It is not essential to take up dyeing in order to make fabric pictures, but it can give some unique qualities to your work and produce effects that are inspiring. There are three reasons that motivate me to set aside some time for dyeing: to fill colour gaps in my fabric collection, to make an atmospheric or dramatic piece of cloth, or to modify fabrics that have some interesting qualities but are perhaps not a very useful colour for my purposes. Personally, I enjoy the fact that you never know quite what will come out of the dye bucket, and often gain inspiration for landscapes, skies and clouds from my tie-dye experiments.

One-pot colour ranges

Although dyeing can be fun, it also takes time and effort so it's good to get 'value' from each bucket of dye – by which I mean an interesting variety of results. The main purpose of dyeing might be to achieve a particular colour, but to make it more interesting, why not throw in a few other experimental bundles? For instance, I have a lot of plain white and off-white fabric with a wide range of textures and weaves that is of limited use to me in its raw state, but which will produce subtle nuances when dyed. I might also cut up clothing and other unwanted fabrics – the fibre content is not always certain but if it looks right it is worth experimenting. A light result is often an indicator of mixed fibre content but may still be a useful addition to your colour range. Patterned fabrics can be totally transformed with a colour change – toning down the pattern in a way that makes it more useful for stitched pictures. A set of the three primary colours should enable you to produce most colours with practice, and manufacturers will often recommend a basic colour range to buy.

Modifying the colour of fabrics

I use fibre-reactive procion dyes on my collection of mostly cotton and silk fabrics. They are simple to use and I can often achieve a range of effects in one bucket of dye. The materials used are readily available and inexpensive: dye, salt, soda, a bucket (ideally white, so that it is easy to see the colour you have mixed), and mixing and stirring equipment reserved for dyeing purposes only. This is not an exact science and can be messy, so old clothes, rubber gloves and some protection for floors and work surfaces will be needed as well as a spirit of adventure. There are plenty of dyeing equipment suppliers on the internet along with blogs, tips and recipes. Always follow the manufacturer's instructions for a successful outcome.

Shibori

This is a whole subject in itself. Material is folded, pleated, scrunched up or twisted around hard objects such as plastic piping before going in the dye bath, resulting in unique patterns. It's easy to do on a small scale with rubber bands and string holding the twists and folds in shape. Although I might use some of the resulting pieces shown below as they are, over-dyeing in a lighter shade of blue may produce even more interesting results. I would use a lot of these pieces for skies and oceans.

The dyeing process

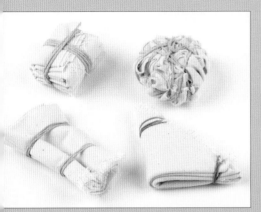

1 To create a variety of dye effects, fold and scrunch up bundles of cotton and silk and tightly bind them with string or rubber bands. These should be washed prior to use in order to remove any 'finishing products' from the fabric, as these can act as a resist to the dye. However, when tie-dyeing, try both washed and unwashed samples – unwashed fabrics tend to result in more defined patterning; the washed fabric results are more diffuse.

2 With fabrics that have been sitting around in your collection for a long time there is not a lot to lose and everything to gain from experimenting with dyeing. Material that has a lot of white in the design tends to be of limited use for fabric pictures, whereas interesting results can come from over-dyeing and filling in the white gaps. Here is a selection of fabrics that I want to modify by dyeing. This includes some previously tie-dyed pieces; they will be washed, dried and refolded before being introduced to each new dye bath.

3 Measure out the correct quantity of cold water in a bucket (calculated in relation to the weight of dry fabric and quantity of dye to be used). Pour in the dissolved dye, then thoroughly stir it in.

4 The bundles and fabric pieces are immersed in the dye. Frequent stirring is needed in the early stages for even distribution of the dye; salt and soda solutions are added over time. The dyeing process takes about 45 minutes but can be left for longer to ensure good take-up of the dye.

5 The results will boost the red section of my fabric library. After coming out of the dye bath the fabrics are thoroughly rinsed, washed, then hung out to dry. The cottons which were not prewashed have come out with some striking geometric patterns generated by folding. Some of these will be dyed several more times to build up a richly coloured fabric. The patterned fabrics with too much white have been completely immersed and resulted in a variety of textured reds. Dyeing stripes and ginghams can often be very effective too.

Using dissolvable fabric

Dissolvable fabric is a thin film of clear or semi-opaque material. Classically, it is stretched over an embroidery hoop in preparation for its use as a support for free-stitching on your machine. When later the film is washed away you are left with a network of stitch created entirely from thread. It can create a lace-like effect or can be more densely worked. Dissolvable fabric has other useful properties when experimenting with techniques and I like to use it in constructing my own 'fabric' from fabric scraps, tangled threads and other odds and ends. Though ultimately held together by a framework of stitch, in construction the dissolvable fabric helps keep all the fragments in place and

enables the machine foot to glide over the uneven surfaces preventing the needle from catching. It can also make sewing delicate fabrics easier by adding a layer of support. Initially, handling it may take some practice and patience as moving your fabric manually beneath the needle while maintaining a steady stitching speed can be difficult. Some buckling up of the fabric is very difficult to avoid and highlights the advantage of making small sections that can then be applied to an embroidery picture. Subjecting a nearly completed piece of work to such vigorous sewing may jeopardise hours of work; much easier to add sections in as a finishing touch. Once your stitching is completed, the dissolvable fabric layer is removed from the surface of your stitching by gentle washing in lukewarm water.

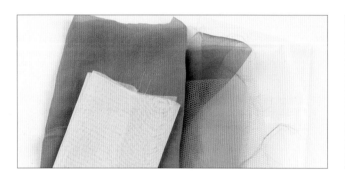

1 In this example, I wanted to create a piece that could be used to form clouds in the sky. I selected some gauzy, see-through fabrics – organza, netting and chiffon.

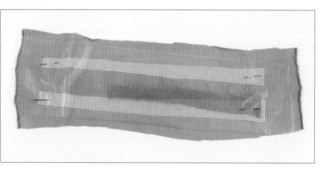

2 Use one fabric as a foundation, then cut strips from the others, layering them on top as an interesting colour base for some free-stitching. Cover with a piece of dissolvable fabric, then pin together.

3 With the feed dog lowered and your darning foot installed on the machine, start stitching. To get the feel of stitching in this way, work your way round the edge of the project, making large stitches. With free-stitching it is you who propels the fabric forwards or backwards, so practise a steady pace and movement. The work is tensioned by holding it between two hands. I haven't used an embroidery hoop as I'm making long thin sections with quite bold gestures.

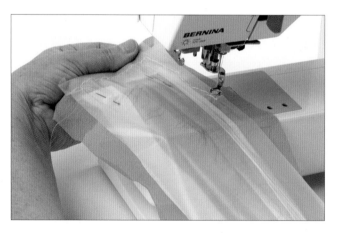

4 Remove all the pins, then work over the surface, trying to create a cloud effect. Move the fabric backwards and forwards, keeping it tensioned between your hands, or work along in small circular rotations. Overwork the fabric in several shades of thread: greys, blues and whites. Start with the darker ones and work towards the lightest.

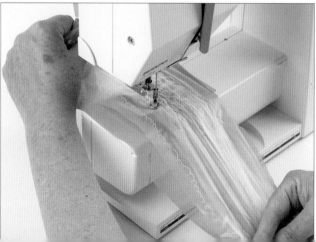

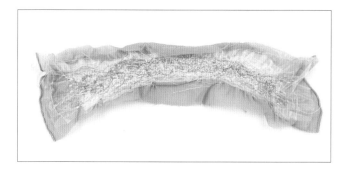

5 This is how your piece might appear after heavy stitching. Using lightweight materials and heavily over-sewing them in this way can cause them to gather and distort, and this is not necessarily detrimental to the finished article. It has reached the point where it is time to check on the results.

6 To dissolve the plastic film, wash it out in several changes of lukewarm water. Roll it up in an old towel to remove the excess water, then leave it to dry flat. Usually any distortion can be teased into shape by ironing on a steam setting. Do protect the work by placing a cloth over it though, bearing in mind that a lot of fine fabrics and thread are synthetic.

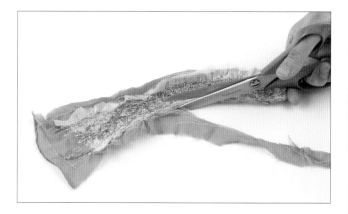

7 Trim away any excess fabric so that you are left with a matrix of textured stitching.

Experimenting

Once you are comfortable with the basic method there are many variations on the same theme. Spend some time developing different motions and rhythms as you move the fabric under the needle. Sewing in a tightly controlled fashion or with more expressive gestures will also give you very different outcomes. Coordinating the speed of the stitching with your hand movements requires skill but will come with practice. Stitch some samples and experiment with a variety of support fabrics. Start with a couple of thicknesses of dissolvable fabric on its own, then try some netting or organza with dissolvable fabric, followed by heavier fabrics. Adding light and shadow with a creative use of thread colour will produce more possibilities. Remember, you can trim and cut these pieces to shape before appliquéing them onto your work.

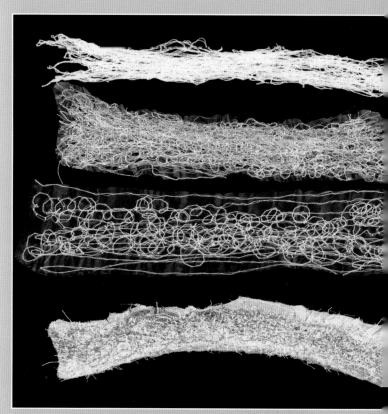

The top example shows white stitching on a double thickness of invisible fabric. After washing out, this leaves you with a construction of pure thread, which is surprisingly solid. It might be used as a bank of white cloud and incorporated into a sky or be part of a seascape. As we work down through the samples, different combinations of stitch movement and base fabric have been used, giving various, versatile effects.

Creating backgrounds

Creating a background can be a good starting point for a picture. Not every piece of work needs to start with a definite idea, and playing around with a colour scheme or patchwork of tiny pieces may be enough to get you started. Having completed a piece of work or spent some time away from creative sewing, doing something free and easy can set you off in a new creative direction.

Using fabric scraps

For this technique, use small scrap pieces of patterned and plain material, along with more interesting and irregular pieces like cut-up samples and embroidery trimmings. Starting with a small square or rectangle, add another scrap by sewing down one side, rotating the piece and adding another and so on, building out from the centre. This doesn't have to be done in a regular fashion and some of the bits added on may be cut from some previously joined fabrics, giving quite a random effect. The aim is to please your eye; go with your instincts on the day and see what results. I always end up adding little pieces on top and use different coloured threads and stitches as the fancy takes me.

In the arrangement of patterns shown above, the resulting piece brings a stylised garden scene to mind.

The background above was built up in a linear fashion using lots of strips trimmed from previous work; these were interspersed with plain colours. A coastal landscape came to mind at this stage so I started to work in features like the hill. Note the use of dissolvable fabric to make over-sewing all these pieces easier.

The bullfinch picture (in progress below, and completed, below right) started life as a very simple arrangement of scrap bag fabrics. One of them already featured a butterfly and that moved me to add a cut-out flower. I squared up the patchwork and sewed it onto a background made from two green fabrics and tried a bird out for size. I then made a branch for the bird and created other vegetation that emerges from the foreground, adding some more flower cut-outs. Lastly, I positioned the bullfinch on his branch and gave him his colourful plumage.

Using found objects

I often find myself in possession of many trivial items that can be hard to throw away: colourful tangles of threads, ribbons, postage stamps, fragments from much-loved pieces of fabric or colourful packaging. An element of nostalgia and memory comes into play alongside the decorative qualities of such items. Over the years I have started to incorporate some of these items into my pictures – a little ritual in my working method. Combining such items with bits and pieces from the scrap bag can be an enjoyable exercise and allows you to reincarnate them into your own fabric; they are all the richer for the personal element contained within. What results may instantly spark an idea for a finished piece of work or alternatively hang around decorating the pin board for a while, waiting to be incorporated into another project. Some pieces may even go through several reincarnations before reaching their final destination.

The process is a fairly quick one: pick out interesting bits and pieces and arrange them by eye onto a square of scrap fabric or interfacing. If necessary, rearrange them to avoid too many thicknesses concentrated in one area, and to ensure that any favourite bits are visible. Pin a piece of dissolvable fabric over the top to keep the arrangement in place for sewing. The stitching can be a methodical covering of the surface or something a bit more random. Bear in mind though that there must be enough stitching to hold all the pieces together when the dissolvable fabric is washed out.

A typical selection of odds and ends that hang around in the studio: sewing thread from my grandmother's work box, a lovely tangle of threads, stamps, ribbon and little pieces of favourite fabrics that I have had for years. The next step will be to apply a layer of dissolvable fabric on top and start stitching.

Some nature stamps set the tone and colour scheme for this sampler (shown complete below and in progress below left), influencing my choice of fabric scraps and thread. As a sort of narrative had suggested itself in the very early stages, this was developed at the stitching stage by suggesting further vegetation and clouds. After washing out, I decided on the addition of a blackbird and with a bit more embroidery my picture was finished.

Background inspiration: before and after

There is an element of 'controlled chaos' in this type of technique; you are guiding the outcome by your choices of colours and fabrics, but by then subjecting it to a stitching and washing process it is altered and transformed into something new that is not completely predictable. During the process, the materials become compacted, the stitching can soften and blend elements together and the whole takes on an interesting tactile quality. It is a more abstract approach that requires some imaginative interpretation of the results. Sometimes this type of experimentation can be very effective when juxtaposed against more figurative elements. Another approach is to develop any themes you have read into a piece by adding more details of the same style.

This arrangement of strips of cloth and tiny tangles of scraps was over-stitched in quadrants; each square spiralling inwards then out again. Post washing and pressing it looked interesting but not a finished piece. After some time pinned up in the studio, the squares of stitching made me think that they might nicely 'frame' a few stamps. I picked out stamps with a bird or landscape theme and grew more branches onto the brown central 'trunk' shape to produce a fabric sampler with an autumnal landscape feel.

Blue fabrics make up the body of this sample with a sprinkling of other colours. The sewing is a simple pattern of backwards and forwards rows worked over the surface. After removal of the dissolvable fabric, a closer inspection reveals that labels and strips of dyeing are incorporated into the piece. Something like this might end up as part of an underwater scene or part of a larger abstract piece.

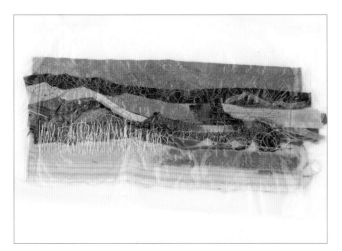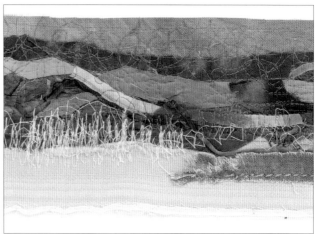

Here, stratified remnants of dyed cloth have been consolidated by applying a layer of dissolvable fabric and free-stitching in a loose, expressive way.

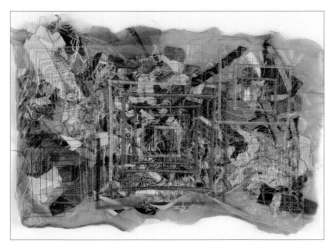

In this experiment I trapped lots of tangled threads and fabrics from the bottom of my scrap bag between a thin piece of blue chiffon and a layer of dissolvable fabric. As it was all very jumbled and chaotic it was over-sewn in coloured grids and squares as a contrast.

Using stitch creatively

It is worth getting to know your sewing machine's capabilities and how they might be customised a little when needed. Making a stitch sampler is a good way to familiarise yourself with what your sewing machine can do. Apart from a straightforward run through of what is on the stitch selector, I would also recommend making some themed samplers – trying out how stitches might be used in different contexts. That might mean seeing which stitches work well for appliqué, or creating a sampler devoted to water-themed effects. I like to think of these pieces as a continuation of the long tradition of hand-stitched samplers – a space for developing stitching skills and ideas. By keeping these to hand or even better, pinned up in the workspace, they serve as a reminder of all the possibilities available to you.

The red sampler pictured below is a basic run through of the stitches in the order they appear on my machine. Even in this case, there are many variations that can be made by varying stitch length and width, and it is a good way of picking up on the decorative potential of some of the 'practical' stitches such as button holes and blind hem stitching.

In the blue sampler below, I experimented with a range of stitches to try to create water-like effects on a piece of tie-dyed fabric. I overlapped rows of the same stitch, sewed a row with the same pattern twice but offset it slightly, and expanded and contracted stitches by increasing or decreasing the stitch length. The bold waves at the top of the sampler were made by pivoting the fabric on the needle as the high and low points of each wave were reached, while varying the width of a close-set zigzag stitch. The lower portion has been free-stitched using a darning foot and with the feed dog lowered, in an attempt to draw a splash and the disturbance of the water.

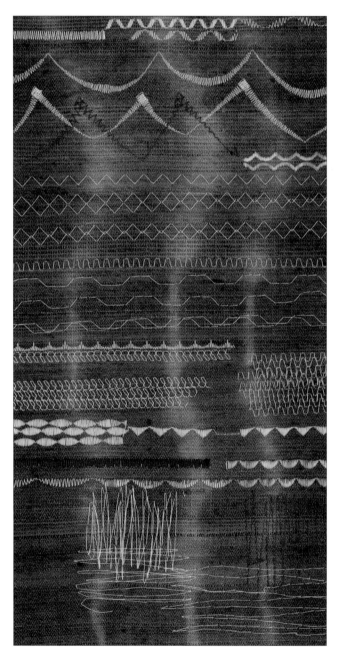

In the sample above, the experimentation continued using a variety of stitches to appliqué some strips of fabric onto a blue background to see what other effects could be produced. I am far from an expert on the great variety of sewing machines available – all I can advise you to do is to practise and become familiar with your own model. The aim is to feel familiar enough with your machine for it to become a dependable tool that helps you express your ideas.

Changing the width of a stitch

I often use the stitch width and length selectors to alter the zigzag stitch setting. Combining the widest setting with the smallest length of stitch creates a solid band of stitching – this is great for a bold outline, for creating blocks of colour or for covering raw edges. Keeping the stitch length very small and working through several different widths will give you variations on this. Making the bold waves on the blue sampler (left) I varied the stitch width as I went along; increasing to, then decreasing from, the crest of each wave. Focusing on the stitch length gives a zigzag that moves from sharp peaks to more flattened, undulating ones, as the length increases. If your sewing machine allows, this sort of adjustment can be done with most embroidery and practical stitches. The results are not always of interest but sometimes expanding or contracting a stitch might just create the effect you need; a sense of distance, or emphasising the shape of an object, for example.

Using the reverse button

There are several functions that I use all the time on my machine, which help me to use stitch as a way of drawing on my textile pictures and taking them a stage on from being just an arrangement of fabric shapes. The reverse button, usually used for finishing off and securing the thread, can be quite an expressive tool with a bit of practice. By using it to repeatedly work backwards and forwards over fabrics, a rich and textured surface can be built up with lots of interesting results. It's a bit like scribbling extra layers of colour over a drawing, and can blend, shade or highlight if the right thread colour is used. Maintaining a steady speed and tension will reduce the problem of gathering and distorting, which can sometimes occur.

Themed samplers

On the following pages are three more samplers, each made with a particular objective in mind. The chicken sampler was a chance to practise the different functions that stitching can fulfil and think about making good colour choices in relation to birds in general. The other two examples concentrate on selecting useful stitches for appliqué and vegetation.

Chicken sampler

Outlining and defining

I used a zigzag stitch around the body of the chicken to cover the raw edges. I used the smallest stitch length, giving a solid line of colour, but varied the stitch width and colour. The colours were selected by my imagining a light source from the right-hand side; the breast is highlighted in a pale shade of brown, the chicken's underside is in shadow and of the darkest shade, while a mid-shade is used from head to tail. The width of this stitching broadens out with the bird's features – broadest at the breast and back and narrowing towards the head and feet. A tapering zigzag is also used to effect on the wings.

Drawn features

Stitching is not just for outlining and fixing fabrics into position. Drawing into the appliquéd shapes with stitching will refine the image. Straight stitching in combination with the reverse button has been used to draw in the contours of the feathers and body shape. On the head, the ruff is stitched using the reverse function in two tones of gold and orange. Use of more subtle colours emphasises where light or shade falls on other parts of the bird. Decorative embroidery stitches have been used very sparingly. I have used only one to give the chicken a speckled breast; varying the thread colour at the same time helped create the effect.

Details

The small features like the beak, crest and wattle make great differences to the character of your bird – it is worth spending some time getting them just as you want them.

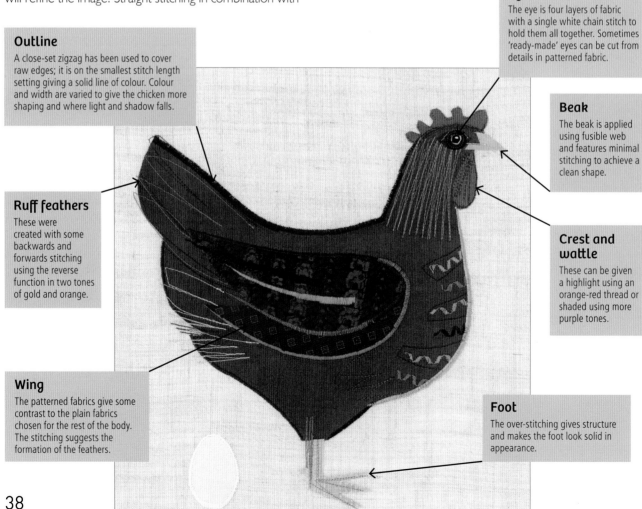

Eye
The eye is four layers of fabric with a single white chain stitch to hold them all together. Sometimes 'ready-made' eyes can be cut from details in patterned fabric.

Outline
A close-set zigzag has been used to cover raw edges; it is on the smallest stitch length setting giving a solid line of colour. Colour and width are varied to give the chicken more shaping and where light and shadow falls.

Beak
The beak is applied using fusible web and features minimal stitching to achieve a clean shape.

Ruff feathers
These were created with some backwards and forwards stitching using the reverse function in two tones of gold and orange.

Crest and wattle
These can be given a highlight using an orange-red thread or shaded using more purple tones.

Wing
The patterned fabrics give some contrast to the plain fabrics chosen for the rest of the body. The stitching suggests the formation of the feathers.

Foot
The over-stitching gives structure and makes the foot look solid in appearance.

Birds in a tree sampler

Here I experimented with lots of different stitches to secure my fabric pieces. As well as the most commonly used zigzag stitch, why not try a four-step zigzag, universal stitch or lycra stitch or any wide, decorative embroidery stitches? Once the tree was made, I went through my stitches looking to select a finer edge for the branches and for stitches that might give a bark texture. I took the opportunity to try out a few vegetation effects on the background; the birds are just for decoration.

Blackbird sampler

In this small picture built up on a scrap bag background, the vegetation is an exploration of what can be done with the stitches on my machine. There are stems of various embroidery stitches, forward and reverse stitched grasses and some free-stitching on the branches. I experimented with different colours and angles of straight stitch to add texture to the birds. The pink flowers were hand-stitched.

Mounting your pieces

The final task is to show your work to its best advantage and put some thought into how it should be presented. Textiles can call for a different approach to framing and don't always need to be put behind glass. Sometimes a softer, sewn solution can be more in keeping with the tactile qualities built up from layers of fabric and stitching. Here are a couple 'low-tech' ways of finishing your work.

Fabric backing

When the stitching is finished, it is unusual to be left with a perfect rectangle or square of work with neat edges. All the layers of fabric and stitching can produce marked differences in thickness, which can make dealing with the edges problematic – too thick in some parts and very thin in others. Simply turning under the raw edges to neaten before sewing may give unsatisfactory results. Instead, mounting the work onto a fabric backing can get around this, and at the same time set off the work to good effect. I would always press a piece of work before framing it, ideally face down on an old towel, with the back protected by a cloth. If during sewing the fabric has sheared in one direction, applying steam while gently pulling it back into shape should rectify the problem. Once this is done, if the edges are very uneven, measure the narrowest point, side to side and top to bottom – this will give you guidance as to the maximum dimensions of your piece. You may wish to crop back a little further than this for aesthetic reasons.

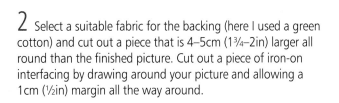

1 Rule out the finished dimensions of your piece of work onto the reverse of the piece with a soft pencil or felt tip. Make sure the corners are square (the grid of a cutting board can be very helpful for this) and ensure that you won't be cropping any details that you want to keep. Use dressmaking scissors to carefully cut the piece to the desired size.

2 Select a suitable fabric for the backing (here I used a green cotton) and cut out a piece that is 4–5cm (1¾–2in) larger all round than the finished picture. Cut out a piece of iron-on interfacing by drawing around your picture and allowing a 1cm (½in) margin all the way around.

3 Iron the interfacing onto the reverse of your backing fabric, then fold and iron in the edges to the dimensions of the interfacing. Trim off any excess fabric to a 1.5cm (¾in) margin. You may want to top-stitch a line of straight stitching close to the edge to give the backing square a good finish.

4 Position your picture centrally and carefully pin it into place. Choosing a decorative stitch (something wide) and an appropriately coloured thread, stitch the picture onto its backing. This could then be further mounted on a canvas block or made into a wall hanging.

Mounting on canvas

Small pictures and experimental pieces can look really effective mounted onto canvas blocks. These are the white primed canvasses used by artists to paint on with oils or acrylic paints, and are readily available from art shops. They come in many shapes and sizes. I find that the chunky ones with deep sides are most effective. You will also need some double-sided tape to have a go at this.

1 Draw round the canvas block, marking its size onto the back of your picture with a soft pencil.

2 Trim your embroidery if necessary and turn in the edges so that they fold along the drawn lines. This can be quite fiddly – keep checking the picture for size against the face of the canvas and adjust if necessary. Use a steam iron to help you with this and make the surface as flat as possible.

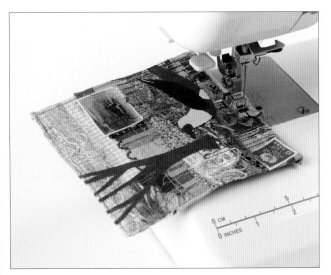

3 Secure the edges by sewing a straight row of stitching all the way round.

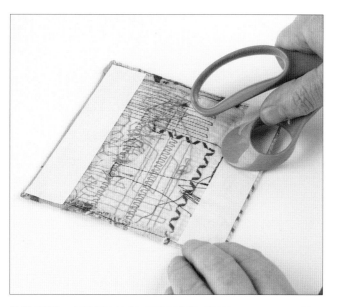

4 Apply double-sided tape to the back of the picture, cover all of the edges and place some strips across the middle. Rub the back of the tape vigorously with a scissor handle or other flat object to ensure good adhesion.

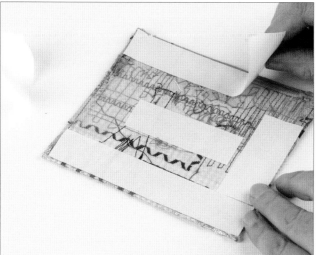

5 Peel off the backing tape and stick your embroidery onto the surface of the canvas block. Turn it onto its face and rub the back of the canvas with your thumbs to make sure it is secure. Weighting it down for a few hours with some heavy books is a good idea. Screw a single D-ring into the centre of the back to hang it up, if desired.

Magpie
15x15cm (6 x 6in)

This was a small experimental piece in which I set a magpie in amongst an arrangement of stamps, tiny fabric scraps and tangled threads using the dissolvable fabric technique.

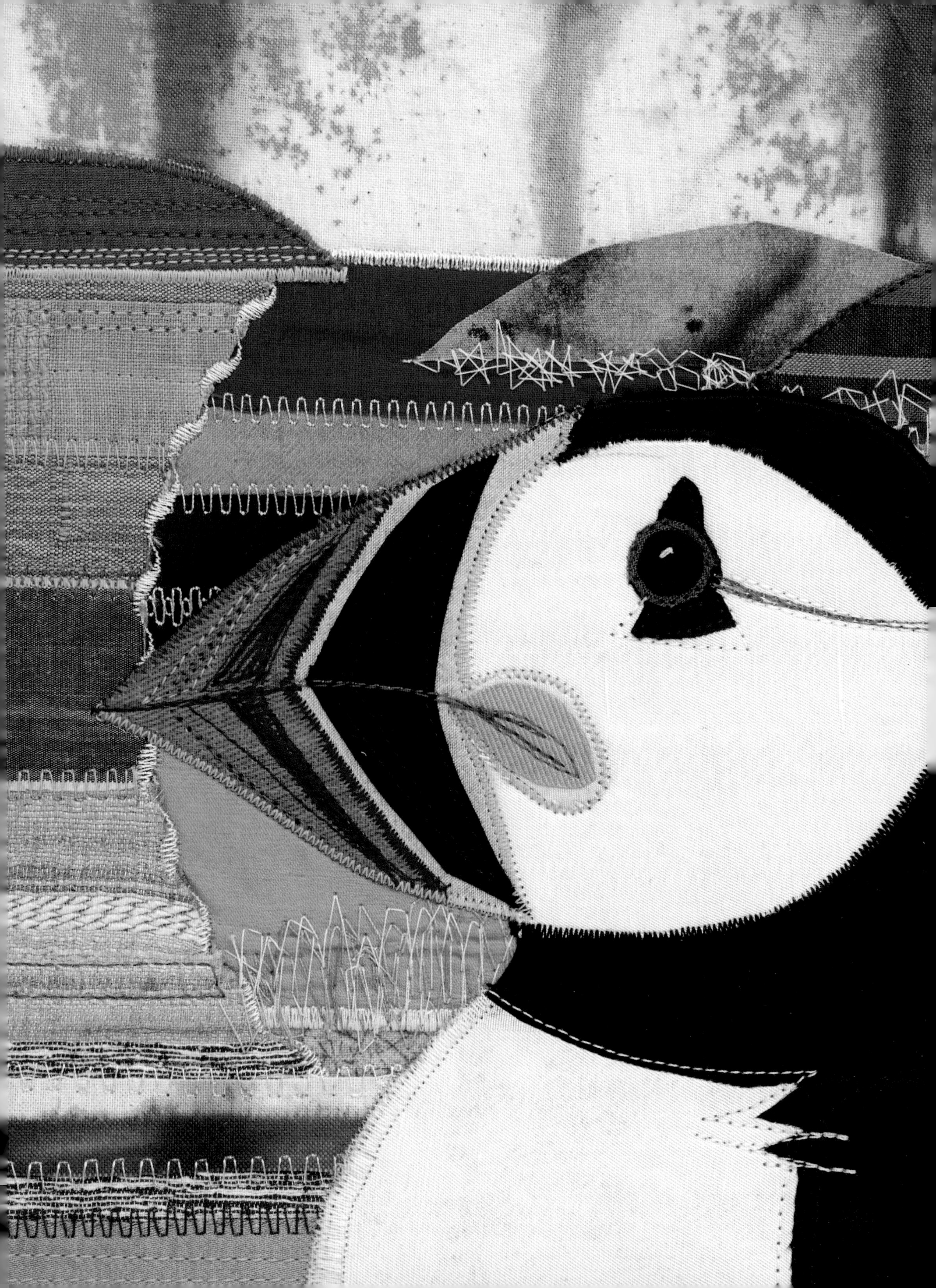

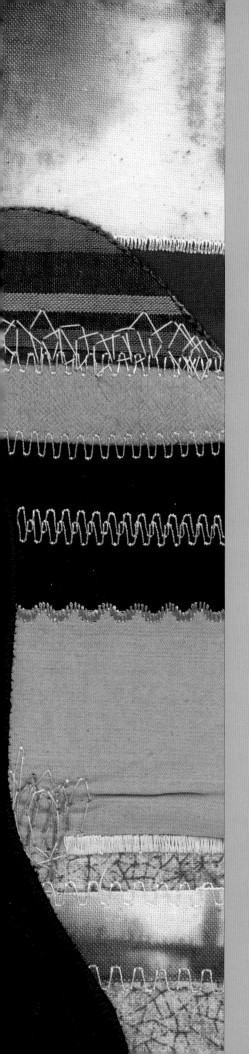

Capturing Character

Birds are engaging creatures and very watchable as they go about their daily business. It is only human nature to place our own interpretation on what we observe in these moments. The plumage, posture, display and group interaction of birds make it easy to invent little characters and scenarios and inspire me to record my reactions to some of these glimpsed encounters. I try to keep the character I am hoping to capture foremost in my mind as I make my pictures, and I hope that the results will resonate with others. It is in the tilt of a head or detail of an eye that a character can seem to be gained or lost. In the following two projects I will show you how to capture the character of two of my favourite subjects: puffins and chickens.

Puffin

Though few of us have seen one in real life, puffins are universally popular and regarded as great characters. Puffins have both a comical and sad appearance: the colourful and striking beak is set against a black and white plumage that bears a resemblance to a formal costume. The large eyes with clown-like markings complete the tragi-comic look. I want the puffin to hold our attention at the centre of a bright, bold image. The strong colour contrasts in the bird's plumage will be offset by a vivid and stylised seascape. This is a simple project, where the background is composed by eye, responding to the fabrics, making them work together, before layering them into a seascape.

Materials
25 x 25cm (10 x 10in) piece of interfacing to use as a backing (this includes a 1cm/½in margin)
18 x 15cm (7 x 6in) piece of interfacing for the shore strata
Fusible web
Your fabric library
A variety of threads

Equipment
Sewing machine
Darning foot attachment
Hand-sewing equipment
Cutting mat and scalpel for templates, see page 123
Tracing paper, pencil and thin card for template making
Fine scissors
Iron and a protective cloth
Sketchbook and paints (optional)

Techniques
Piecing fabrics
Machine embroidery, appliqué and free-stitching
Hand-stitching
Dyeing fabrics (optional)

1 Using my bird scrapbook (which contains several puffin pages) I selected a puffin and made a preliminary colour sketch. The composition is a stylised one: the puffin looms up filling the foreground; the coast has a flattened perspective and there are billowing clouds in the distance.

2 To adapt the sketch for making a textile picture, I drew out a square the same size as I want the finished piece of work to be. The sketch is simplified right down to outlines of the component features and I have accentuated the flattened perspective.

3 Gather together a collection of fabrics: you will need bright blues for the seascape, along with a selection of browns, yellows and greens for the shore. For the puffin you will need a white fabric, a black, and a blue-black or very dark grey as well as two tones of yellow and an orange.

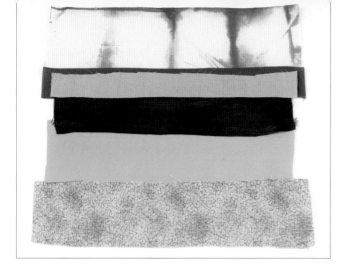

4 On top of your backing material, arrange a few strips of fabric to build up layers of sea and sky. When you have finished, the backing should be completely covered in blue fabrics. Iron the fabric strips in place.

5 To create the shore, cut out another piece of backing, 18 x 15cm (7 x 6in) in size. In the same way as you did for the sea and sky, build up an arrangement of fabrics for your shoreline. These should be narrower than the blues: between six and eight overlapping fabrics is probably about right. Use the shoreline template (page 123) as a guide to roughly gauge how your fabrics will work. When you are happy with the arrangement, iron it down and pin down any loose strips.

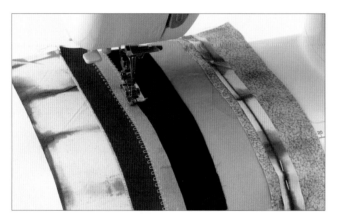

6 Stitch down the layers using decorative stitches that help to suggest waves and different textures in the sea. For the sky I added a dramatic piece of shibori (tie-dyed) fabric. An off-cut of this fabric is repeated further down, mirroring the sky in the sea. This will breach the shoreline so should only be pinned in place at this stage.

7 Stitch the shore strata area into place, covering the raw edges. Apply a rectangle of fusible web to the back, then trace off the shoreline from the template (remembering to do it in reverse if you are drawing it on the back). Cut out the shape.

8 Lift the pinned shibori strip out of the way and iron the shoreline in position; lay the strip back down and stitch it in place along both long edges. I added a sand dune and two small islands in the distance, stitching them in place as shown (see also pages 49, 50 and 51). Use a darning foot and lowered dog feed on your sewing machine to create some waves breaking against the rocks and close to the shore.

9 Where the shore meets the sea, add a wavy stitch in white to finish off the edge and suggest waves breaking.

10 Back all your puffin fabrics with fusible web. Trace off all the templates (see page 123) and cut out the pieces using small sharp scissors. It may help to lay them out in the order shown. Starting with the whole head and body shape in black, position the white breast and head pieces before removing their backing paper and ironing them down. The dark grey shoulder piece follows next. Now move on to the beak, ironing the yellow component into place followed by the orange which aligns over the fore end of the beak. Finally the black arrow shape sits on top of the yellow beak section and the deep yellow leaf-like shape is ironed in place. Assemble the eye separately in order of ascending size; black pupil onto red disk onto black background. Iron each layer in place as you go.

11 Remove the backing from the eye and iron in place. It is important to do these stages with great care, making sure it looks right before ironing each layer down. Finish off the eye with a single chain stitch in white thread, giving a white highlight to the pupil.

12 Iron the puffin in position. It is good practice to use a cloth to protect your work from the risk of marks or displacement of delicate pieces. Sew detail into the puffin's eye and beak using a variety of stitches and threads, and sew around its body (see right and pages 50–51 for more detail).

Tip
Have a practice run using the templates and coloured papers if you are not confident about how all the pieces are put together. A pair of tweezers or a dressmaking stiletto are good tools for nudging small pieces into the exact position required.

48

The strip of dyed fabric creates a dramatic sky without need of further embellishment. Beneath this, a variety of stitches is used to suggest waves. Much of the stitching also fulfils the dual function of neatening raw edges as well as decoration.

Where shoreline meets sea, the juxtaposition between blue against yellow and offsetting of the stripes and stitching create an interesting effect. I deliberately chose quite textured fabrics for the shore.

A lot of fine zigzag stitching is used for outlining (and securing) the shapes. Using slightly different shades of thread from the base colour can be very effective, for example, a bluish white down the front of the white breast would imply a shadow and helps give shape to the bird. I have also drawn into the bird (for example the eye detail and on the neck and shoulder) following its contours to again give it more shape. Subtle shades of orange and red are used to give the effect of the ridges on the beak.

Chickens

Chickens are great characters and display very individual traits. In this project they are out and about on a blustery day, all on their own mission but at the same time keeping an eye out for what everybody else is up to. The pecking order must be maintained! To create the sense of movement and spontaneity, the background is impressionistic with one or two landmarks added in. This is the free and easy part of the project using trial and error to build up a layered landscape. The chickens themselves are cut out using templates; the choice of fabric and detailing will bring their individual characters to life.

Materials

30 x 30cm (12 x 12in) piece of iron-on interfacing
Fusible web
Dissolvable fabric
Your fabric library
A variety of threads
Scrap bag materials

Equipment

Cutting mat and scalpel for templates, see page 124
Tracing paper, pencil and thin card for template making
Fine scissors
Pins
Sewing machine
Iron and cloth
An old towel
Hand-sewing equipment

Techniques

Piecing fabrics
Using dissolvable fabric
Machine embroidery, appliqué and free-stitching
Hand-stitching

1 Assemble a good selection of fabrics; collect together small strips from your scrap bag as well as larger pieces. Think sky, earth tones and greens when making your selection. Cut a good selection of strips in preparation for creating your background.

2 Take your square of interfacing and start by creating a base layer in just two colours. At the top, position an 8cm (3¼in) deep piece of blue fabric; beneath this place a 22cm (8¾in) deep green piece. Iron them into place. Now start to imagine the landscape, breaking up the blocks of colour by layering strips of fabric over the top. Introduce some earth tones at the bottom of the picture, a couple of hills in the background and give some interest to the sky.

3 To bring this all together and create a stable background, lay a sheet of dissolvable fabric over the top, and pin it in place. Sew carefully round the edge; this will help keep the fabrics in place. The pins can now be removed. Work over the whole surface with your sewing machine. Have some fun experimenting; you can follow the contours of the landscape, be random or sew in a geometric pattern. Changing the thread colour will also add interest and texture. In this example there is some stitching following the contours of the hills and linear stitching across the sky. Lower down the fabrics were crisscrossed in several directions.

4 Gently wash out the stitched and layered fabric in several changes of lukewarm water to remove the layer of dissolvable fabric. Roll up in an old towel to remove the excess moisture, then leave to dry flat.

5 Continue to work on the foreground details; add some bushes. The branches are a simple arrangement of strips in several tones of brown. It's good to cut these from scraps with fusible web on the back; they can simply be ironed into position. Otherwise, pin them in place ready for sewing.

6 Select three or four shades of brown, ochre and green thread. Starting with the darkest shade, work over the top of the shrubs, stitching backwards and forwards. Use the reverse button if you have one. Repeat the process working up through the colours and creating lots of tiny branches radiating out from the tree.

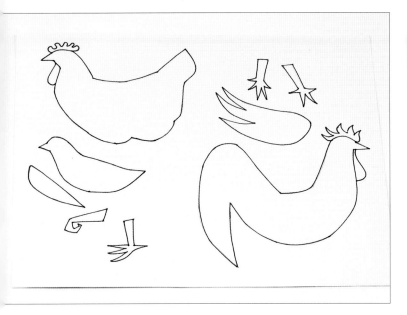

7 Make the templates for the chickens: see page 124. Use a light-weight, flexible card.

8 Select your chicken fabrics and prepare them by backing them with fusible web. Trace around the templates and then cut out all the pieces.

Tip

Too much pattern can confuse the eye so err on the side of caution by only using simple patterned fabrics. If you want to use some patterned fabrics for the chickens, alternate a patterned fabric with a plain one: put a patterned wing on a plain body or vice versa.

9 Assemble the eyes by cutting out tiny black circles. Apply them to a yellow fabric and then cut out as a slightly larger circle giving you a black pupil with yellow surround. Cut a red lozenge (think of a leaf shape) for each eye to sit on.

10 Iron down the red base for the eye on both the chicken and the cockerel's heads. Hand-stitch a single chain stitch with white thread through all the layers. Iron the wings into place on all three birds.

Tip

Remember to work from the background to the foreground. Once you have cut out and assembled the chickens (to body and wing stage) try them out on your background and see where you want them to overlap in relation to each other and the landscape. Make some markers with a tacking stitch or soft pencil.

11 The cockerel is the first to be ironed down and stitched into place. The wing and eye already in position, there are the comb, legs, beak and extra tail feathers to add. The tail feathers and beak are cut out from scraps. Once in position, embellish with some stitch. The neck plumage is simple forward and reverse stitching in a golden yellow, burnt orange and dark maroon. Start with the darker shade and work to the lighter one. Using the same colours a fine tapering zigzag adds some variety to the tail and wing (see pages 57 and 58 for more detail).

12 Position the speckled hen against the cockerel and bushes so that her head overlaps him slightly.

13 Remove the backing paper and iron the hen in place, ready for her finishing touches.

14 Add stitch detail to the hen's wing feathers. Use a variety of stitch types and colours (see pages 57 and 58) to give texture and colour.

15 Use your sewing machine to 'draw' feather shapes over the tail and wing. Then outline the hen with a close zigzag stitch: I used maroon on her top and front, and black underneath, for variety.

16 Place the chick in the foreground with its juvenile wings flapping. Very simple running stitch is used to emphasise the movement. Use a selection of colours to give a sense of depth (see right). Also outline the bird's body using a close zigzag stitch.

Tip
Give a lot of care to how the legs, eyes and beaks sit. These features give a lot of the character. Try moving them around a bit and you will see the difference!

The cockerel close-up shows the feathers that have been added
to the tail and wing using scraps of fabric and over-stitching.
Straight stitching is used to anchor the crest, beak and eye.
The bright neck feathers were created using three shades of thread.
The hen is outlined with a very close zigzag stitch. It can be
increased or decreased in width to accentuate the hen's shape.

The chick brings colour and life to the bottom of the
picture. Apart from outlining the body with a closely
stitched zigzag to give him definition and prevent the
raw edges fraying, I have used forward and reverse
stitching to give a sense of movement.

This way of making a background gives rich textures and colours. The bush and branches add yet another layer. With the layering of fabric and overstitching there is not much need for decorative stitches. I have used a little to suggest vegetation on the hill top.

Sparrow

30 x 30cm (12 x 12in)

This is a stylised still life featuring a bowl of cherries, some figs, a pot of flowers and a visiting sparrow. The flattened perspective and simple representation of the fruits and bowls are in contrast to the more detailed bird. Underlined by a shadow, the bird looks as if it has just alighted and will soon depart. The inspiration was the colours and sights of summer and in particular the pleasures of eating outdoors. It features appliqué with machine and hand embroidery.

Lapwings
42 x 30cm (16½ x 12in)

This is a scene from a regular walk. It is always a pleasure to see these shy, elegant birds when they visit the local fields. The background is composed of dyed and modified fabrics with appliqué and machine embroidery.

Smallholding
46 x 61cm (18 x 24in)

A band of free-range chickens and a strutting cockerel are out foraging. In the distance there are ducks on the pond and a fox lurks in the shadows. The techniques used include dyeing, appliqué with free-stitching, machine and hand embroidery.

The Visitor

22 x 22cm (8¾ x 8¾in)

This background was an exercise in putting together some squares cut from a piece of discarded silk painting and other 'precious' scraps of material. Some of the flowers were embroidered over and then more flowers and vegetation added in. It provided the backdrop to a little encounter between two birds taking place in a secluded corner of a garden. It was embellished with more machine and hand-stitching.

The Fountain

24 x 24cm (9½ x 9½in)

This was another assemblage of tiny material scraps that suggested a garden to me. The two goldfinches and vegetation bring our attention right to the foreground and at the same time frame the ornamental garden scene with cascading fountain behind. The work features a pieced background with appliquéd birds and vegetation with machine embroidery.

Greenfinches
20 x 20cm (8 x 8in)

The branches of a tree displaying the first signs of spring provide a perch for a pair of greenfinches. Through the network of branches a whitewashed building can be spied in the distance. This multi-layered landscape is overlaid with appliqué and stitched branches and birds.

Swifts

25 x 25cm (10 x 10in)

A bird's-eye view over a patchwork of fields and flowing river as a pair of swifts perform their aerobatic feats high in the sky. The techniques used include dyeing, appliqué and machine embroidery.

Depicting a Scene

In this chapter the theme is seeing birds in the context of their surroundings. Often to get this across some 'artistic licence' is needed, as capturing birds in a landscape brings with it the technical difficulty of the subject being small in comparison to its backdrop. You may need to be creative with angle and perspective in order to represent the scene that inspired you. Translating a memorable moment into a textile picture can involve quite a few processes: jotting down the idea, taking a photo of the setting, using reference material to research the birds, and bringing this all together in a working sketch. Here are a couple of projects showing ways to approach this.

Seagulls on a Boat

This is a scene from a regular walk of mine. There are several things at play here to catch the attention: the parade of seagulls on the boat evenly spaced but all striking different attitudes, the reflection of the boat on the water, which almost looked like stitch in the photo, and then there is the estuary itself. A photograph taking in the whole scene didn't really reflect the impact experienced in real life; the birds and boat were lost in the distance when they had been the focus of attention at the time, and the coastline seemed insignificant. Here is my textile interpretation bringing all the elements I enjoyed to the fore.

Materials

Iron-on interfacing, 28 x 42cm (11 x 16½in: this includes a 1cm/½in allowance)
Dissolvable fabric, 30 x 8cm (12 x 3¼in: with shrinkage allowance)
Hand-dyed fabrics (optional)
Organza for the boat's reflection
Your fabric library
A variety of threads

Equipment

Cutting mat and scalpel for templates, see page 124
Tracing paper, pencil and thin card for template making
Sewing machine
Fine scissors
Pins
Iron and cloth
Hand-sewing equipment
Sketchbook and paints (optional)

Techniques

Piecing fabrics
Using dissolvable fabric
Dyeing (optional)
Machine embroidery, appliqué and free-stitching
Hand-stitching

1 Plan the layout using photographic reference. I decided to bring the boat closer to the viewer, include some landmarks from the far shore and feature the shimmering reflection, combining elements from different sources.

2 Once the basic outline is in place, develop your ideas with a colour sketch or painting, to make sure that the composition will work.

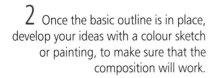

3 If there are elements of your design that need a little more practice or experimentation, try them out. Here, I sketched out some seagulls in different stances.

4 With your photographs and sketch at hand, gather together fabrics to fit in with the landscape colour scheme. Hand dyed materials seem to lend themselves to this project.

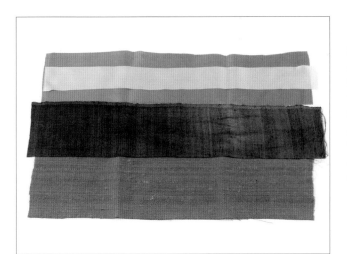

5 The base colours are divided into three equal horizontal sections: light water at the bottom, dark water in the middle and sky at the top. Iron the three base colours into place on your piece of iron-on interfacing. The lighter strip is the foundation for a cloudbank. This can be ironed into place using a strip of fusible web adhesive. In the final piece this arrangement will translate into water with reflection in the foreground, water and the seagull boat in the middle ground, and landscape and sky in the top section, with each of these occupying about a third of the space.

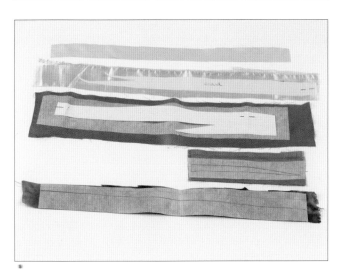

6 Using the land and cloud templates on pages 124–125, trace off the shapes onto paper. Pin these to the backs of the landscape fabrics ready for cutting out. Fusible web adhesive has been applied to smaller pieces and delicate fabrics for ease of use.

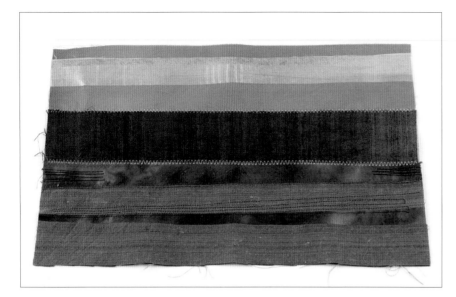

7 Work some detail into the sea and sky. Stitch over the raw edges with a decorative stitch or zigzag set to look like waves. Some backwards and forwards running stitch will create the feel of ebb and flow in the water. Two dyed satin bands have also been sewn in (this was one strip of fabric cut diagonally in two, one wider than the other) to add interest to the sea and break up the rigid divisions. A layer of pale grey added to the cloudbank gives illumination to the sky.

8 Using the darning foot and lowering the feed dog, work on the cloudbank with free-stitching. Use circular and backwards and forwards motions to build up your clouds.

Tip

Using several subtle shades of colour will greatly enhance your cloud effect. Here I have used a pale blue, blue-grey and a silvery grey. Start with the darker shade, then refine it with a lighter one, repeat, ending with highlights from your palest shade.

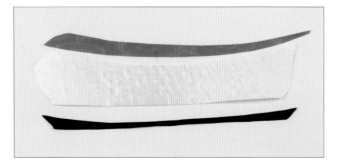

9 Using the boat template on page 124, cut out the white base fabric and the blue and black strips from fabrics that have been backed with fusible web.

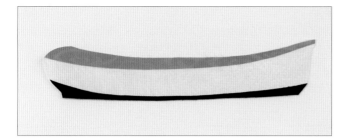

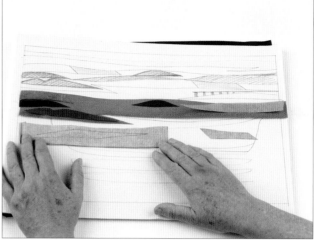

10 Position and iron the blue and black strips into place on top of the white piece, remembering to leave the backing intact on the base fabric. Set aside.

Tip

It may look as if quite a lot of effort is wasted stitching areas that get covered at a later stage. The reasoning behind doing it this way it is that it allows freedom of movement and flowing lines where working round obstacles would be restricting and technically difficult.

11 Using your original sketch for guidance, assemble the landscape, starting at the top; use templates A–I on page 124 to create the field and dune shapes from fusible web adhesive-backed fabrics.

12 Arrange your landscape pieces on the backing fabric, slightly overlapping the cloudbank. When you are happy with their placement, iron them down.

13 Here you can see the basics of the landscape in position and ready to machine embroider. The cloudbank sits on top of the hills and illuminates the top section of the picture.

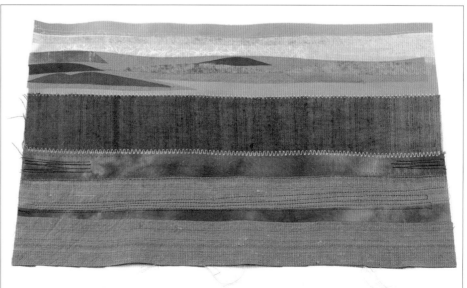

14 Develop patterns in the fields using straight stitching and tones of green and brown. For the trees and hedges, employ more textural stitches; varying the width of close zigzag stitching is also effective. See pages 76–77 and page 78 for further detail.

Tip

A transparent embroidery foot for your machine can be a good investment when doing this sort of detailed work.

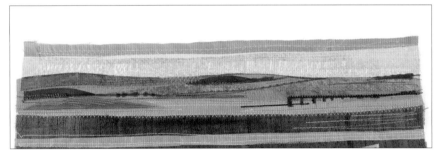

15 When you are satisfied with the landscape, the sandbank and jetty can be added. The jetty is embroidered over a fabric sandbank.

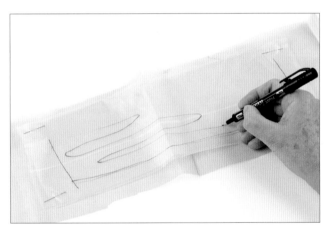

16 For the boats' reflection, which will occupy the foreground, use free-stitching on an organza base. Top a double layer of blue organza with dissolvable fabric and pin together. Use a felt tip to draw in the area of shade.

Tip

The technique shown in step 17 tends to bunch up the fabric in an irregular way, making accuracy difficult. Cut the organza and dissolvable fabric with a generous allowance to compensate for this. The reflection can always be trimmed down to size if it turns out too big (as it was in this picture).

17 Using white, mauve and warm grey threads, move the fabric rapidly backwards and forwards under the needle to create the reflection. Quite a density of stitching is needed for this. The shading is worked in last. Wash out the dissolvable fabric in lukewarm water and dry flat. Iron on a low heat setting, protecting your work with a towel. Trim away the excess organza.

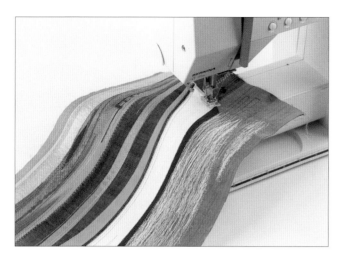

18 Secure the reflection in position with white running stitch, running it back and forth over the whole area. I also used the white running stitch to improve the slightly irregular shape of the reflection. Iron the boat on top and stitch in a few details on top (see pages 76–79 for further detail).

19 Draw out some simple seagull shapes on fusible web-backed fabrics. Use two or three different qualities of white to give subtle variations. Do the same for the wings; find two or three fabrics to cut your wing shapes from.

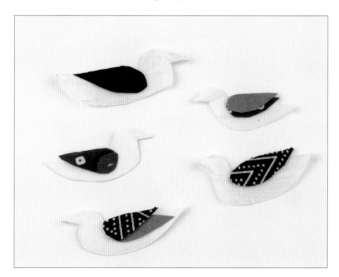

20 Iron the wings into position on the birds' bodies. Assemble a selection of seagull shapes and wing combinations.

21 Try out different arrangements before ironing into place. Remember to leave a space between the bodies and the boat for the legs of the birds who are perched.

22 Add some extra detail to some of the wings using white embroidery thread and long backstitches (see finished image, right, for more detail). The mooring rope is another nice finishing touch: sew a wavy line across the front of the boat, using your machine. Back a few scraps of yellow fabric with fusible web, then cut out a selection of small triangular beaks. Iron them in place as shown, on a selection of the gulls, then outline them with a couple of hand stitches using yellow or orange embroidery thread.

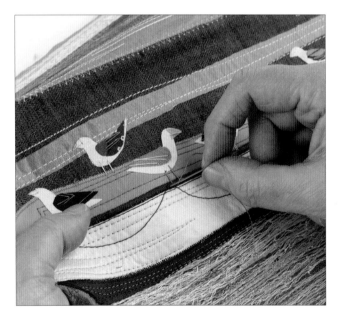

23 Hand-stitch the gulls' legs in place using orange and yellow embroidery thread and small backstitches.

Tip
The free-stitched reflection is backed by organza as this 'disappears' into the background, making it look as if it was stitched in situ. Such heavy sewing directly on the piece would most likely have caused buckling of the fabrics and potentially spoiled the picture.

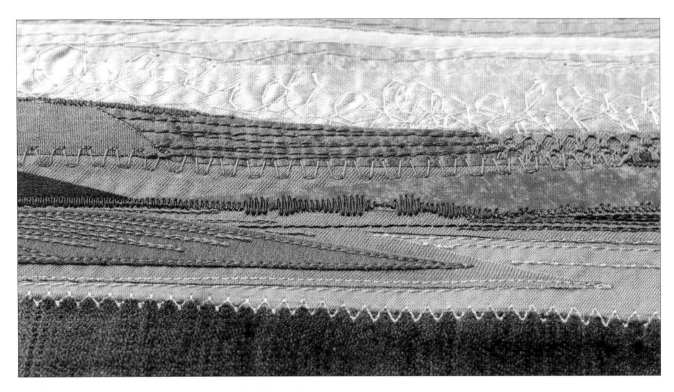

Free-stitching for the cloudbank is contrasted against straight stitching and decorative stitches for the fields and vegetation. Note the width manipulation of the zigzag in green to give a line of bushes.

The outline of the boat has been zigzagged to cover raw edges and a dark rim added at the juncture between blue and white. Drawing some contour lines in the black, white and blue sections creates a more convincing boat. Quite a lot of detail went in to making water effects in the early stages of the picture.

More of the landscape detail. The jetty pillars are different widths of zigzag and follow the line of the shore; the jetty is topped with a blanket stitch. Underlining the boat with a dark row of stitching makes it sit well in the water.

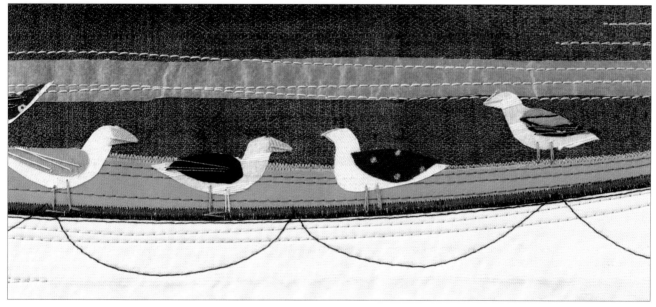

The seagulls are given character by variations in fabric and shape. Legs and beaks are hand-stitched.

The trimming from my free-stitching was used to good effect making it look like the current is breaking up the reflection. A little overstitching in white also helped. Moving a couple of seagulls to the foreground also improves the composition, leading the eye to travel up through the picture.

Blackbirds

Blackbirds glimpsed in the garden or out on a walk provide me with a lot of entertainment. A new player on the scene is much cause for hopping about and striking an attitude. The way territorial disputes are resolved in a comic dance without any harm other than a few ruffled feathers could be a lesson to us all! I have made a series of embroideries featuring such encounters. The scene is set on a domestic scale; a little patch of ground contained within the garden.

Materials

Iron-on interfacing, 30 x 30cm (12 x 12in)
Scrap bag fabrics
Your fabric library
A variety of threads

Equipment

Cutting mat and scalpel for templates, see page 125
Tracing paper, pencil and thin card for template making
Sewing machine
Fine scissors
Hand-sewing equipment
Sketchbook and pencil (optional)

Techniques

Piecing fabrics
Machine embroidery and appliqué
Hand-stitching

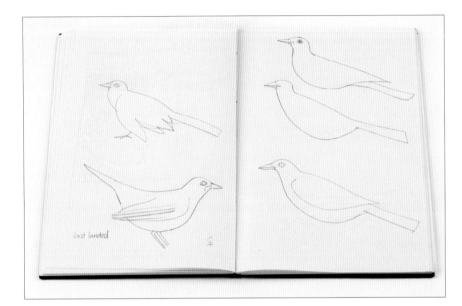

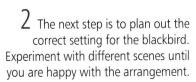

1 For this project you can use my blackbird shape, given on page 125, or create your own. To create your own design, follow steps 1 and 2; otherwise move on to step 3. Make quick sketches of blackbirds in action, or even work from photographs – become familiar with drawing out the shape of the bird.

2 The next step is to plan out the correct setting for the blackbird. Experiment with different scenes until you are happy with the arrangement.

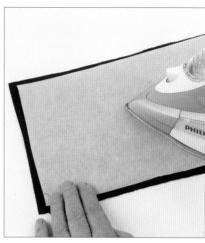

3 Select and trace off a blackbird – see page 125 or use your own design. Use this shape to create a template from light-weight cardboard (an old breakfast cereal box is ideal).

4 Prepare a rectangle of black fabric that is large enough to fit two of your birds by ironing a sheet of fusible web to the reverse.

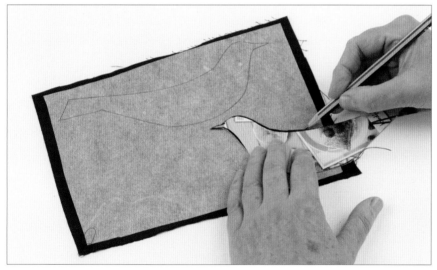

5 Trace the two birds onto the back of your black fabric. Start by tracing off one complete bird. For the bird on a branch, simply turn the template to the reverse and trace off the front half of the bird. Put the bird shapes to one side for the moment.

6 The next stage is to create the garden backdrop. A variety of vegetation, the pathways, ornamental trees, pond and sky need to be represented. Select your fabrics with care, considering how the textures and patterns might work together.

7 Lay down the square of interfacing first, then start to arrange your fabrics on top. Here the aim is to make a simple, stylised representation of a garden: 'beds' of colour are arranged round a central 'lawn'. I used three bands of blue as the starting point for the sky.

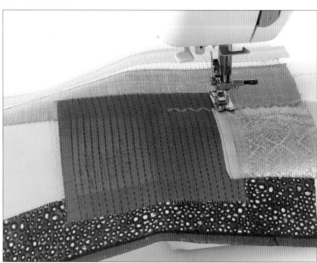

8 Continue to tweak your arrangement until you are happy with the balance of colours and textures. With the square now entirely covered, iron the fabrics in place.

9 Stitch around the shapes to secure them and add decoration, and add borders using some decorative stitches.

10 Here the initial layout of the garden scene is complete, ready for the next level of detail to be added.

11 Next I added gentle slopes and distant trees to the skyline. Cut out a pond for the middle distance and iron into place. The pathway that bisects the lawn is assembled from lots of fragments of material backed with interfacing (a trimming from a much larger piece), but any suitable fabric will do. The ornamental hedge is a block of paisley shapes cut from sari fabric.

Tip

Getting the sequence right when making a fabric picture is very important; the basic principle is to work from far distance to near. For example, the pond is partially obscured by the hedge, and the stems of the hedge rest on the pathway, so the order of work is pond, pathway, and then hedge. It's a way of thinking your way around a picture that will be acquired with practice.

12 Stitch some detail onto the new garden elements. The distant hills need some variation and layering. A close zigzag stitch can make hedge-like boundaries, and varying the width as you sew can create an irregular tree line. Use two or three different shades of green to maximise these effects. Experiment with other stitches on your machine. A distant hill has also been added and secured with extra stitching (see pages 87–89 for further detail).

13 Sew around the path with decorative stitching; don't be afraid to use contrasting colours – here I used blue and orange – before zigzagging some stems for the hedge plants. I have used a slightly different colour for each plant.

14 Make each stem originate high in the tear-drop shape. Draw some branches into each plant shape. Forward and reverse stitching in straight stitch is good for this.

15 Add further little touches like a surround to the pond and a patch of bright water; the foreground 'earth' has been broken up by a strip of vegetation on which one of the birds will stand. Ensure the background is exactly as you want it before you add the blackbirds' branch. In keeping with the rest of the picture, the branch is a simple shape. It was cut from off-cuts of fabric already backed with fusible web.

16 Iron the branch in place as shown. Stitch all the way along the branches and add a bit of shading in places (see pages 87 and 88 for more detail).

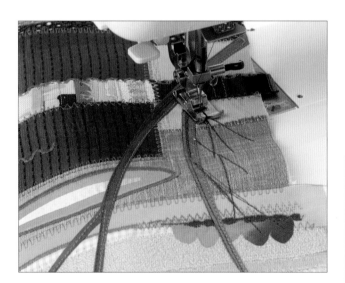

Tip

Think of the fine branches as lots of long elongated stitched 'V' shapes. Sometimes they can be a series of joined-up shapes. Using different coloured threads and overlapping each layer of 'V's will disguise how they have been made.

17 Using two shades of green and a brown, stitch on a network of branches. Start with the dark green, followed by a light brown and finally a bright green. I used simple straight stitch, machining forward and then using the reverse button, pivoting the work when the stitch reached the end of each branch or main stem.

18 The garden and landscape is ready for the blackbirds.

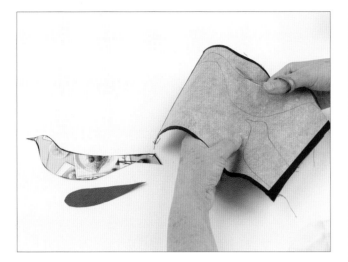

Tip

The wings of each blackbird can be cut out in a different quality of black from the main body (usually a lighter one) to give some subtle variation.

19 Cut out your blackbird pieces. Prepare the eyes and wings. Position the birds as you want them before removing the protective backing and ironing them into place. How they stand in relation to each other is the key to the success of the picture.

20 Stitch round the bodies and wings using a close zigzag. Work into the neck, wing and tail feathers to show the lay of the feathers using straight stitch. Apply the eyes and beaks (see pages 87 and 89 for further detail).

21 Cut out a pair of legs for the bird on the ground, and position them with careful attention to the stance of your bird.

22 Iron the legs into place.

23 Sew the legs in place with straight stitch and a light yellow thread; use the machine to 'sketch' in some simple detail on the foot (see pages 87 and 89 for further detail).

24 Change to an orange thread and sew the backs of the legs and draw in more detail on the feet. Cut two scraps of fabric to form the legs of the bird in the tree (see right for reference). Machine sew each leg in place: I used yellow thread for the right leg and orange thread for the left, but choose the colours as you feel suits your work.

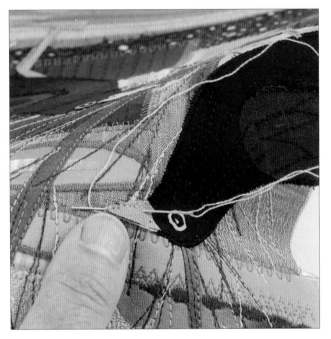

25 Cut out the beak shapes and secure them in place with a small 'V' of machine stitching on each bird.

26 Finish each beak with a couple of large hand stitches to give it more definition.

Choose your colours of both thread and fabric carefully: the network of fine branches worked in three colours creates a three-dimensional look. The wing in a different texture of black fabric is much more effective than a uniformly black bird would be. Also note the feather detail worked on top in straight stitch. The positioning of the white highlight to the eye (a French knot or single chain stitch) makes sure the eye stays in position and gives it more expression.

A close-up showing some of the stitches selected for assembling the patchwork of fabrics. On the bird, the close-stitched zigzag outline can be varied in width to either blend in or accentuate. Different coloured threads can be used to draw the plumage.

Stems and branches for the ornamental hedge are all given slightly different treatments. Straight stitch and a tapering zigzag have been used.

Swallows
28 x 30cm (11 x 12in)

A summer scene where young swallows on flying practice use a mast as a resting place; the adult birds swoop in attendance. This is a simple treatment of a coastal scene using bold, simplified shapes. The use of hand-dyed satins helps to create a luminous sea and sky on a sunlit day. Techniques include appliqué, free-stitching and machine embroidery.

Green and Gold
27 x 37cm (10²/₃ x 14²/₃in)

A trio of finches moving around the tree branches on the periphery of a garden. The viewpoint is looking from the shadows into the light. This patchwork garden is made using fabrics in earth tones with textured natural fibres, with appliquéd branches and birds and machine stitching.

Clovelly Chickens
50 x 50cm (19¾ x 19¾in)

Out on a walk one day I was met with the surprising
sight of two chickens perched on a high gatepost,
which was topped by a cairn of pebbles. To give
impact to the picture I have made a full-on view of
the scene with brightly coloured chickens emerging
from the dark vegetation. I used hand-dyed fabrics
with appliqué and machine embroidery.

Chicken Run II

30 x 30cm (12 x 12in)

A light-hearted piece recording the birds and animals
occupying a rural landscape; in particular the
chickens as they wend their way home to roost. It
features a pieced background using modified fabrics,
appliqué, free-stitching and machine embroidery.

Blossom

20 x 20cm (8 x 8in)

This was a holiday moment captured in textiles. A pair of busy blue tits are feeding off the insects on a peach tree in blossom. This piece uses layered fabrics with cut-out and appliqué flowers, and hand and machine stitching.

Magpie
13 x 13cm (5¼ x 5¼in)

This is a tiny embroidery, with an experimental background made using dissolvable fabric and free-stitching, incorporating stamps and tangled threads.

Shoreline
100 x 50cm (39½ x 19¾in)

One of my regular coastal walks passes through a habitat for curlews, brent geese and shelduck, amongst other birds. As one walks, light reflected on the water is constantly changing, fragmented by weather and the ebb and flow of the tide. The birds shift in and out of focus. The impressionistic background was composed from small strips of fabric sewn onto a backing, with appliqué birds and landmarks and overstitched with machine embroidery.

Telling a Story

In these two projects, two very different images are created but they are both about creating a narrative. The Seagull on the Beach captures the essence of a holiday afternoon. No great event took place watching the seagulls and sailing boats on this lazy afternoon; it is more about how it felt. I have freed myself from trying to represent a particular scene and gone for an evocation of a summer's day. Bird Ark tells another sort of story: I was inspired by words, asking the question what an ark for birds would look like. This gave free reign to the imagination and the creation of a little universe with its own rules and characters. All sorts of stories can be read into it by both maker and viewer.

Seagull on a Beach

This simple scene captures a seagull perched on a rock, waiting for the tide to turn. The beach is quiet and the sea calm; this peaceful scene caught my eye one afternoon. Simplifying a scene can give it more impact: here, the aim was to recreate the mood rather than a precise landscape. There are no complicated techniques employed in this project. It is a demonstration of using the properties of your fabrics to their full effect. When I work like this, with an idea in my head, much of the designing is done 'on the page', with the handling of the fabrics generating many of the design ideas.

Materials

Iron-on interfacing 22 x 22cm (8¾ x 8¾in)
Fusible web
Your fabric library
A selection of threads

Equipment

Cutting mat and scalpel for templates, see page 125
Tracing paper, pencil and thin card for template making
Sewing machine
Iron and ironing cloth
Scissors
Hand-sewing equipment
Sketchbook and paints (optional)

Techniques

Piecing fabrics
Machine embroidery
Hand-stitching

1 Here is a quick colour sketch I made of the seagull. I liked the way he was perched and remained motionless for some time on his rock as if taking in the scene around him. Various boats bobbed in the distance. At this stage I made sure that I blocked in the main colours and added in a few details.

2 You will need to select fabrics for the sea, sand, sky and seagull. I chose lots of bright fabrics with rich, contrasting colours; I picked out a careful balance of patterned and plain material as well as a selection of whites, blacks and greys for the seagull.

3 Create the sand, sea and sky sections. Cut and position three bands of fabric on your 22 x 22cm (8¾ x 8¾in) square of iron-on interfacing: here my brown sand and blue sky base pieces are each 11 x 22cm (4⅓ x 8¾in), while the blue sea piece is 3 x 22cm (1¼ x 8¾in).

Tip

Base fabrics will be held in position by the interfacing. Top layers should be applied with fusible web or pinned into position ready for sewing.

4 Introduce the impression of texture and light on the sea by layering some blue patterned fabric and a silver grey satin.

5 Continue to layer up strips of fabric in the sand and sea. A bright contrast in the sand and a rivulet of water in the foreground breaks up the solid blocks of colour.

6 Iron the fabrics onto the backing, protecting them with a cloth as you do so. Alternatively, pin them in place.

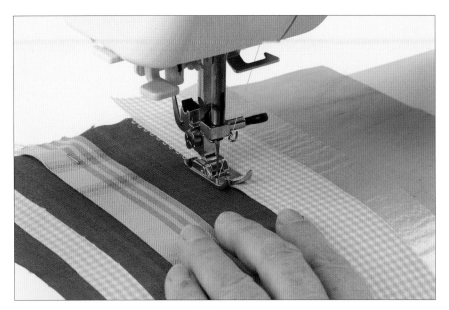

7 Sew along the edges of each of the strips. Use decorative stitches on your sewing machine to cover and neaten raw edges and break up solid blocks of colour. Experiment with stitches and thread colour.

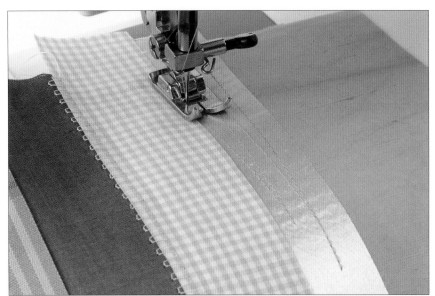

8 On the satin fabric, sew backwards and forwards using straight stitch to help blend in the colours and create interest.

9 The blue textured fabric made me think of how undercurrents create darker waters around coastal features.

10 A sandbank is added and will give the picture more structure. We now have sea and sky colours brought down onto the beach. The sandbanks make the beach colours travel up into the sea and sky, balancing the composition.

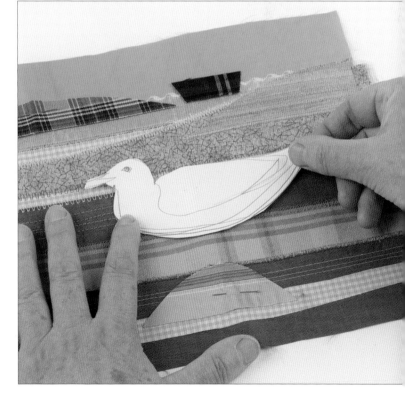

11 Now is the time to tackle the seagull. It won't be stitched into place for a while but as the central character, we need to see how it fits into the picture and what other elements we might wish to include. Use the template on page 125 to create and cut out your bird in paper, and check that you are happy with how the size works.

Tip

Use your scrapbook cuttings or reference books to get your seagull shape if you haven't done a sketch or don't want to use mine. Practise drawing some seagulls onto scrap paper until you are satisfied you have the right shape and size.

12 Use the template or a cut-out of your own sketch to draw round as a guide and cut out the body shape from a white fabric backed with fusible web.

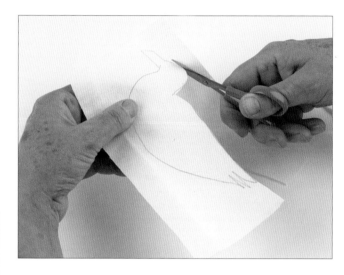

13 Cut out the other bird parts from fabrics backed with fusible web – see the templates on page 125. Choose a selection of greys to make up the wing. You can see below how I selected my colours.

14 The pieces are assembled and ready to be ironed down.

104

15 At this point, stand back and assess the balance of your work. I decided that I needed another sandbank in the top left corner, and I also added a rock for the seagull to stand on. Remove the backing from the bird and iron it down.

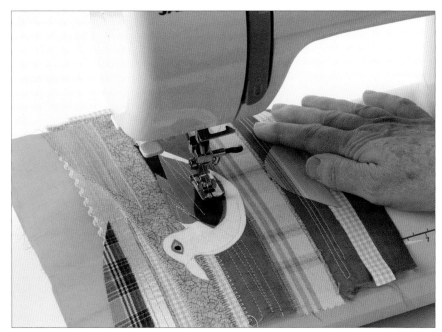

16 With some silvery grey thread, work over the wing and back to produce the feather shapes (see also pages 107 and 108 for more detail). Using more machine stitch 'draw' into the rest of the body, giving some shape to the head and shadow on the breast.

17 Using the reverse button, stitch backwards and forwards across the seagull's rock to secure it and make it appear more rounded. Add a back leg to the seagull: simply iron then sew a strip of fabric into place as shown. Consider the colour before you sew it down: by using a darker fabric than that of the front leg, it will appear to recede into the background (you will attach the front leg in step 18). Stitch a yellow beak into place, covering the white (see also pages 107 and 108).

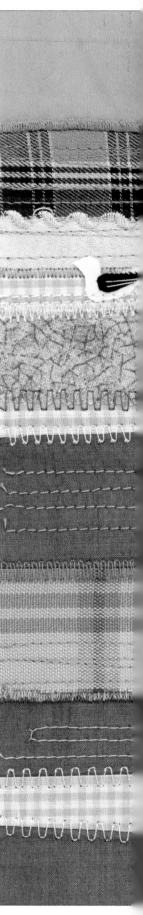

18 Cut out a yellow front leg using the template on page 125. Stitch it in place using a dark orange thread to define the webbed feet and a bright yellow to highlight the leg.

19 Continue to add in stitched details: more detail is added into the background; some swimming seagulls and sailing boats. In the foreground a decorative stitch in blue creates waves lapping against the seagull's perch.

Tip

Once all the basic elements are in place, take some time to step back from your work. It can be good to put it away until the next day and see it with fresh eyes. Does anything jar? Is anything missing?

Stitching across and through the blocks of colour creates more interest than just following the cut-out shapes. I am trying to create the contours of the bird by 'drawing' more detail over the top. On the white body there is a satin fabric highlight, which has been over-sewn with off-white thread following the light and shadow on my sketch. The wing and back contours mimic the lay of the feathers and unite the different greys. The final touch is to do a little hand-sewing: a single chain stitch in white to highlight the eye, and a few stitches to the head and beak.

Wave effects have been created using various stitch settings and an appropriate thread colour; they also cover raw edges at the same time. A close-set zigzag stitch can also be used to great effect: the tapering zigzag on the stone makes a shadow. Behind, using different thicknesses and colour of thread, the zigzag softens the line between the different fabrics. A running stitch in lighter or darker shades also helps to blend the fabric colours and produce subtle effects.

The bright boats add a focal point, inviting the eye to travel up through the picture. A wavy stitch creates a lively sea. The sandbank is an interestingly textured raw silk worked into with some yellow thread.

Bird Ark

This project was inspired by a question that popped into my head while looking at some of my previous work involving arks: what would an ark for birds look like? The idea took a hold on my imagination and after a few sketches I arrived at the idea of a bird-shaped vessel sailing forth full of birds of all shapes and sizes. Having created this little scenario, a narrative was built around it; the birds shelter in a nest rather than the hold of the ship, a branch from the nest forms a makeshift mast and so on. The notion of the journey was also important: travelling through the night amongst the waves.

Materials

Medium-weight iron-on interfacing, 40 x 40cm (15¾ x 15¾in): this includes a 1cm (½in) allowance all the way round for ease of handling

Dissolvable fabric, 45 x 10cm (17¾ x 4in) – this was trimmed to 40 x 5cm (15¾ x 2in) after shrinkage

Your fabric library

A variety of threads

Fusible web

Equipment

Sewing machine

Dressmaking scissors and small sharp pointed scissors

Hand-sewing equipment

Cutting mat and scalpel for templates, see pages 126–127

Tracing paper, pencil and thin card for template making

Layout paper and pens

Techniques

Appliqué

Free-stitching

Dyeing (optional)

Hand-stitching

Piecing

1 I started with an initial sketch, working out how my ideas could fit together on the page.

2 Leaving out all the finer details, I next made a basic layout on tracing paper. This step can be especially useful for larger and more detailed pieces. Use the template elements on pages 126–127 to create your own.

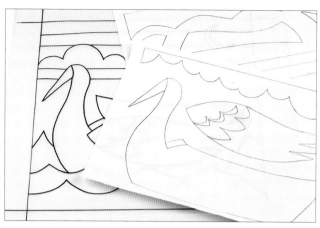

3 Trace this simplified layout onto your 40 x 40cm (15¾ x 15¾in) square of interfacing. Trace the layout onto it using a felt tip, with the adhesive side of the interfacing upwards.

4 Using a few sheets of layout paper, trace off the individual elements ready to cut out and use as patterns.

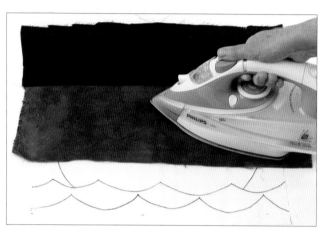

5 Select likely fabrics from your collection. Think about the atmosphere and colour scheme as you choose. Make a broad selection initially to give yourself plenty of choice. Assess how the different fabrics work together as well as their suitability for individual components.

6 Using your layout as a guide, measure off two large bands of fabric for the sea and the sky backgrounds; iron them in place.

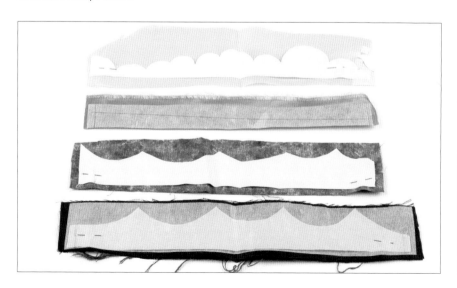

7 Iron fusible web onto the back of a few strips of sea and sky fabric. Pin or draw your sea, sky and cloud pattern pieces onto the back, ready for cutting out.

Tip
If using delicate or light-weight fabrics likely to fray, backing them with fusible web before cutting out makes tracing, cutting and securing a lot easier.

8 Cut out the waves, clouds and other elements.

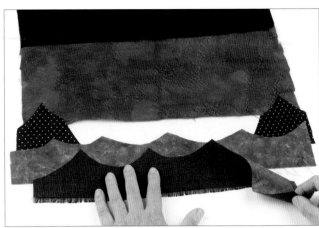

9 Position the waves. The top tier can be ironed into place; lightly secure the bottom two tiers at their base using stitch or pins. This is to allow the bird ark to be inserted later. You will have some interfacing showing; do not worry, as this will later be covered by the bird ark.

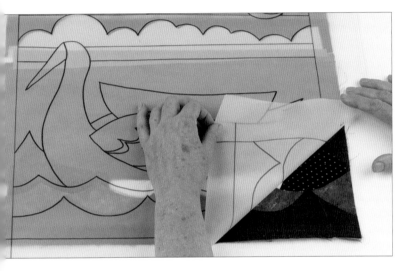

10 Use the layout tracing to help you position all the background elements correctly, as shown.

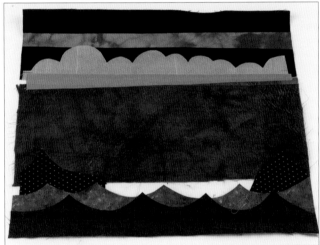

11 Iron all the sky elements in place. Create your ark shape and wing using the templates on page 126. Cut them from fabric backed with fusible web; I used a soft grey taffeta fabric.

12 Work up the sea and sky with some decorative stitch. I have done some free-stitching on the clouds to soften their outline and other decorative stitching to accentuate the effects of moonlight on the scene. The moon is created from a disc of dark tie-dye with a crescent of silver satin applied. Its outline is circled with some dark blue satin stitch, then rings of running stitch.

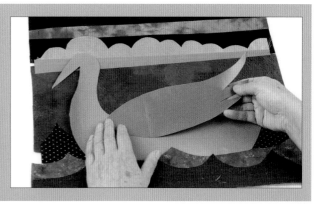

13 Iron the ark in place and secure
the breast and tail end with tapering
satin stitch and some running stitch
suggesting feathers (see page 115 for
more detail). To create a foamy sea, use
the techniques shown on pages 30–31
to create a band of fabric using free
machine stitching on dissolvable fabric
and layers of voile. Cut it to shape if
necessary and position it amongst
the waves.

14 Using the templates on page 126 and scraps of material
already backed with fusible web, create the bird's head. Start
by cutting out a black head and neck shape and apply it to
the base silver fabric. Next put the red 'cap' and white eye
stripe into position, removing their backing papers and ironing
them into place. Assemble the eye separately, starting with
the smallest piece: black onto yellow onto black. Remove the
backings (apart from the black base fabric) and iron the top
two layers down; trim to shape if necessary. Remove the final
backing and iron the eye into place. Lastly cut and apply the
beak. Over-stitch the head and neck to create feather effects
and blend the colours (see pages 115 and 116).

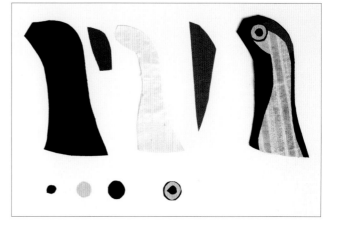

15 Cut out the nest shape from your chosen fabric backed with fusible web. Allow a good margin to the base of the nest to give some flexibility when positioning the wing. Peel the backing paper away from the nest base. Trim leaving a 2cm (¾in) strip of backing in place at the top so that the birds' heads can be inserted later. Using the layout, position the nest and iron it in place.

16 Start embroidering the branches. Select three or four brown and green shades of thread for the branches. A close tapering satin stitch makes effective branches. Start with the branch 'mast', which I ruled out using a soft pencil to guide me. Other branches have been done by eye. Again, leave the top edge of the nest clear at this stage, concentrating on the background and lower foreground twigs. Final touches to the nest will be done when the birds are in place.

17 Use the templates on page 127 to cut out your pairs of birds. Start with the cranes and peacocks and work into the foreground, arranging the shapes. When you are happy with your nest of birds, remove the backing paper from the inside of the nest and iron everything down. You can now finish the branches on the nest allowing some to overlap the birds.

18 The birds need just a few finishing touches to give them some character – most of this is done with machine stitching; white running stitch for the cranes' breast feathers and the detail drawn into the beaks, for example. The eyes are hand-sewn – a tiny chain stitch often encircled by another one in a deeper or lighter shade. Chain stitch is also used for the peacock's crest and the breast markings are created using short stemmed fly stitch. Use your imagination to add little details for the crests, eyes and beaks. See page 116 for detail.

19 Trace off the four wing pieces. You need a whole wing shape in soft grey, a darker grey top wing, which is overlaid with a gold organza, and raspberry organza detail. Assemble using fusible web or stitch.

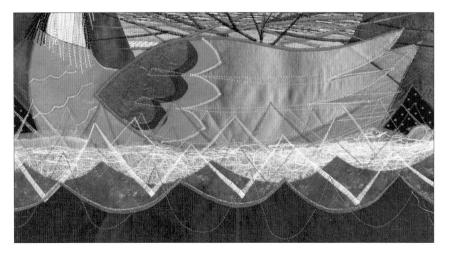

20 Carefully position the wing, hiding the lower part of the nest, and stitch it in place. Add more stitching to give the impression of plumage: select some blue, grey and white threads. Starting with the darker shades, make some bold wave shapes using a tapering satin stitch against the ark. Do a second and third row in lighter colours and increasing size, moving down towards the foreground. The final touch is to work in between these rows with a looping running stitch in different colours, to create a lively sea.

Getting the sequence of sewing right can be quite challenging. In this case, the background branches must go down first, then the tallest birds are applied, with the smallest in front. The addition of beaks and eyes is a delicate operation and it's easy to displace them when embellishing with stitch, but this is also the fun part when the characters finally come to life. Once the birds are completed, the branches of the nest are extended upwards and outwards, unifying this part of the picture.

Over-stitching with greys and whites on the clouds and crest helps create the impression of moonlight illuminating the scene. Drawing into the appliqué shapes with a well chosen thread colour can produce lots of subtle effects and details. The bird perched on the head was a small finishing touch; his bright pink wing bringing a burst of colour to this part of the picture.

The moon is cut from some of my tie-dyed fabric for the dark side, with a crescent of grey satin appliquéd over the top (the same as my cloud fabric). Giving it a dark edge helps give it a rounded appearance – I have varied the width of this stitching: broad on the dark side to fine against the light, to increase this effect.

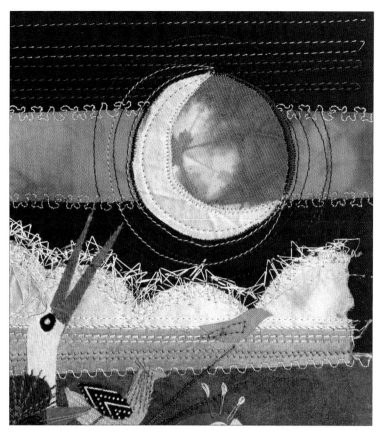

You can see below the simple treatment of the wing – the edges are stitched with a close-set zigzag that tapers towards the wing tips. The wing is drawn into with straight stitch, suggesting the formation of the feathers. The waves too are a combination of a tapering zigzag matching the rise and fall of the waves with rows of straight stitching in between. The variation in thread colour is important, helping create depth and movement; here three shades were offset against one another.

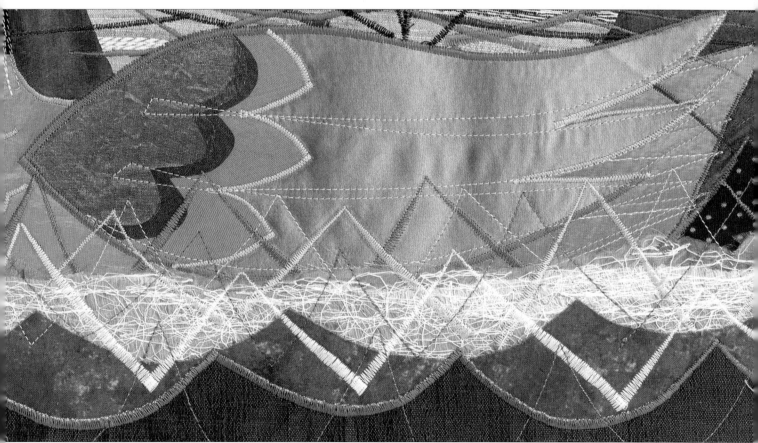

Chorus

24 x 24cm (9½ x 9½in)

This picture records some of the birds I encountered when walking down a local lane. The background is pieced together from my scrap bag. The sky includes some hand-dyed fabrics with free-stitching. The birds and branches are appliquéd and machine embroidered. The tree unifies the picture; the formation of the birds echoes its triangular shape.

Harvest Jug
60 x 80cm (23²/₃ x 31½in)

An embroidery inspired by the anonymous work of a craftsman-potter from the past (see also page 19). The naive decoration of birds and flowers on the jug has been translated into brightly coloured flowers and a pigeon, in a fantasy that attempts to capture the freshness and simplicity of the original. The piece features appliqué with machine embroidery.

Discovering the Dodo
90 x 110cm (35½ x 43¹/₃in)

With only naive portraits and faded museum specimens as inspiration, I decided to work hard on giving this dodo some wonderful plumage in order to bring it alive. The simple arrangement of dyed fabrics that forms the background helps bring our attention to the fore, leaving no doubts as to who is the star of the show. The piece features hand-dyed fabrics with appliqué and machine embroidery.

Doubtful Sound
60 x 80cm (23¾ x 31½in)

This was a commission piece celebrating a memorable trip to New Zealand,
in particular the dramatic scenery and the wildlife encountered on a cruise
through Doubtful Sound. This piece employs hand-dyed fabrics, free-stitching on
dissolvable fabric, appliqué and machine embroidery.

Pie in the Sky

30 x 30cm (12 x 12in)

This garden scene developed from a composition of a circle and four rectangles. It conveys a well-kempt and ordered environment. The arrival of two restless, noisy magpies in the garden breaks up the formality and dominates the scene. Hand-dyed fabrics, free-stitching, appliqué and machine embroidery are used.

Chicken Run

50 x 50cm (19¾ x 19¾in)

A roving band of chickens is at the heart of this rural scene. The cockerel stands sentinel while the chickens are out and about foraging. There are farm buildings and a patchwork of fields. This started life as a sort of crazy patchwork, where I was trying to combine some bright red, pink and orange patterned fabrics with a batch of modified fabrics over-dyed with a vibrant green. To make it work as a landscape it needed some device to pull it all together. The tree seemed the perfect solution and provided a home for more birds. The techniques used include hand dyeing, free-stitching, appliqué and machine embroidery.

Templates

Bird in Flowerbed templates, shown at 50 per cent of actual size; see pages 23–25.

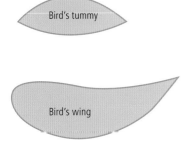

Bird's tummy

Butterfly

Flower

Bird's wing

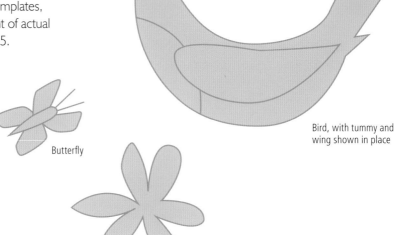

Bird, with tummy and wing shown in place

Puffin templates, shown at 50 per cent of actual size; see pages 46–51.

The four parts of the puffin's beak

The three parts of the puffin's eye

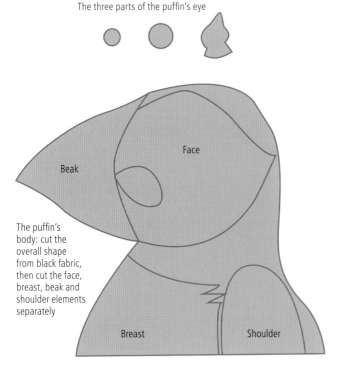

Beak

Face

The puffin's body: cut the overall shape from black fabric, then cut the face, breast, beak and shoulder elements separately

Breast

Shoulder

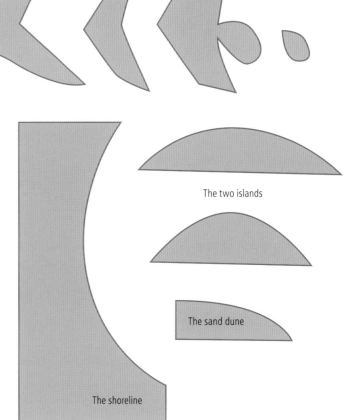

The two islands

The sand dune

The shoreline

123

Chicken templates, shown at 50 per cent of actual size; see pages 52–59.

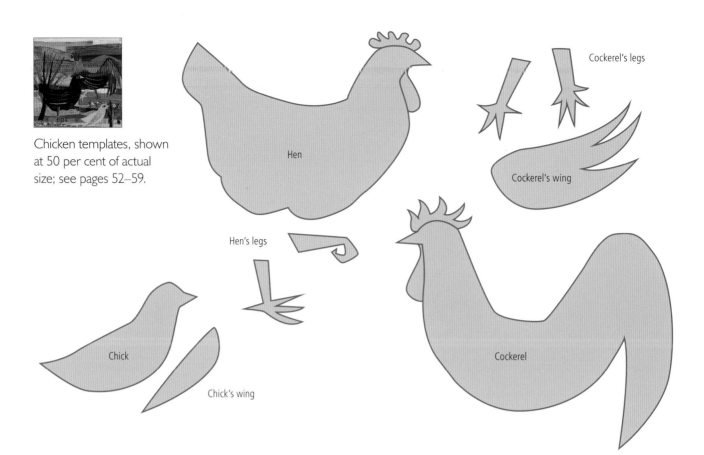

Cockerel's legs

Cockerel's wing

Hen

Hen's legs

Chick

Chick's wing

Cockerel

Seagulls on a Boat templates, shown at 50 per cent of actual size; see pages 70–79.

Background elements: I have given a suggestion of colours to use, but choose whatever fabric scraps you have in your stash

A: light green

B: light green

C: dark green

D: mid-green

I: dark green

G: mid-green

E: pale green

H: mid-brown

F: beige

The boat: cut the overall shape from white fabric, then cut the top part from blue and the bottom part from black

Seagull

Seagull

Seagulls on a Boat templates,
shown at 50 per cent of actual
size; see pages 70–79.

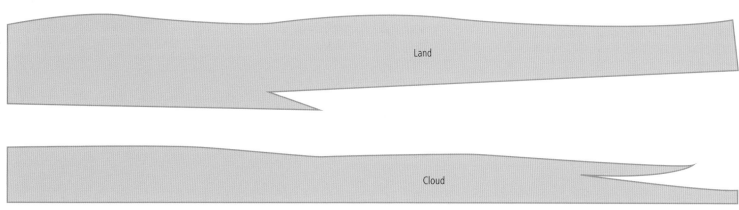

Land

Cloud

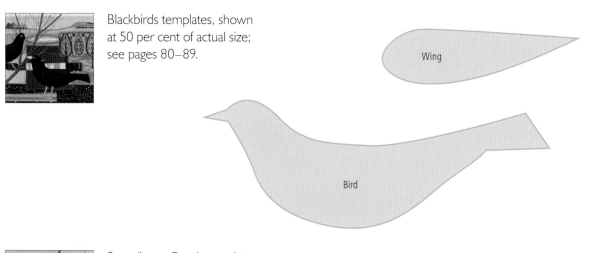

Blackbirds templates, shown
at 50 per cent of actual size;
see pages 80–89.

Wing

Bird

Seagull on a Beach templates,
shown at 50 per cent of actual
size; see pages 100–109.

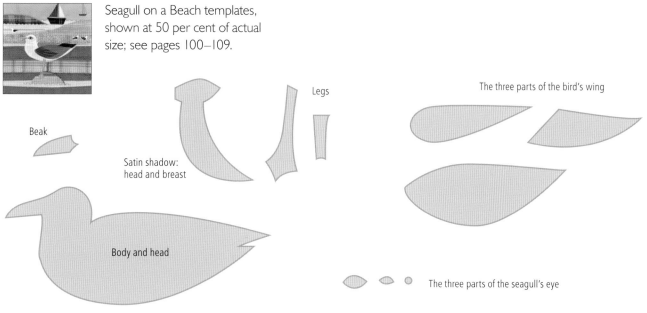

Legs

The three parts of the bird's wing

Beak

Satin shadow:
head and breast

Body and head

The three parts of the seagull's eye

Cloudbank: shown here upside down

Wing

Ark

Three coloured wing pieces

Bird Ark templates, shown at 50 per cent of actual size; see pages 110–117.

The three parts of the bird's eye

Bird's head and neck pieces

Beak

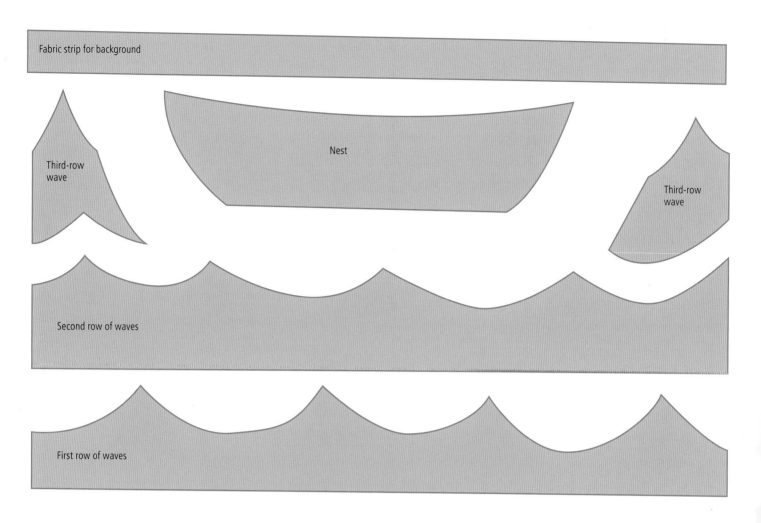

Fabric strip for background

Third-row wave

Nest

Third-row wave

Second row of waves

First row of waves

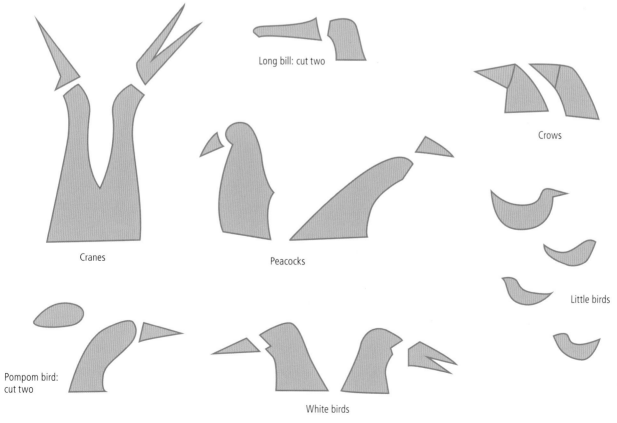

Long bill: cut two

Crows

Cranes

Peacocks

Little birds

Pompom bird: cut two

White birds

Index

Bideford Seagulls
24 x 24cm (9½ x 9½in)

I glimpsed this scene from the top deck of a bus. The rain was pouring down and a group of seagulls had perched in formation on the ribs of an old boat, awaiting a turn in the weather. Bideford Long Bridge and the old town gave a great backdrop to the moment. The piece features appliqué and machine embroidery.